Reading Instruction and Assessment

Understanding the IRA *Standards*

Bonnie B. Armbruster

University of Illinois at Urbana-Champaign

Jean H. Osborn

University of Illinois at Urbana-Champaign

Allyn and Bacon

Boston ■ London ■ Toronto ■ Sydney ■ Tokyo ■ Singapore

Series Editor: *Aurora Martínez Ramos*
Series Editorial Assistant: *Beth Slater*
Executive Marketing Manager: *Amy Cronin*
Production Editor: *Kathy Smith*
Editorial-Production Service: *Chestnut Hill Enterprises, Inc.*
Composition and Prepress Buyer: *Linda Cox*
Manufacturing Manager: *Chris Marson*
Cover Administrator: *Kristina Mose-Libon*
Electronic Composition: *Cabot Computer Services*

Library of Congress Cataloging-in-Publication Data

Armbruster, Bonnie B.
    Reading instruction and assessment : understanding the IRA standards /
Bonnie B. Armbruster & Jean H. Osborn.
      p. cm.
    Includes bibliographical references (p.) and index.
    ISBN 0-321-06395-3
    1. Reading—Standards. 2. Reading—Ability testing. 3. International
Reading Association. I. Osborn, Jean. II. Title.
LB1050.46 .A77 2002
428.4—dc21   2001026672

Printed in the United States of America
10 9 8 7 6 5 4 3 2 1   06 05 04 03 02 01

CONTENTS

CONTENTS

ABOUT THE AUTHORS

Bonnie B. Armbruster obtained her MA and PhD degrees from the University of Illinois. For several years she was a Senior Scientist at the Center for the Study of Reading at the University of Illinois, Urbana-Champaign. She is currently a Professor in the Department of Curriculum and Instruction. Her area of specialization is reading and writing in the content areas, or reading and writing to learn. Dr. Armbruster is the author of more than fifty articles and book chapters. She has served as a consultant to several major textbook publishers. Dr. Armbruster teaches reading and language arts methods courses for elementary education students as well as reading, writing, and children's literature courses for graduate students. She also has an interest in service learning and works with the America Reads program at the University of Illinois.

Jean H. Osborn is an educational consultant. With Bachelor's and Master's degrees from Stanford and the University of Illinois, she has had a variety of experiences as an administrator, a researcher, and a teacher. She was a member of the Center for the Study of Reading at the University of Illinois, Urbana-Champaign staff for almost twenty years, serving as Associate Director for twelve years. Prior to that, she worked as a field consultant for the United States Department of Education's Follow Through program. In this capacity she worked as a staff development leader, classroom consultant, and developer of language arts curricula. She is the coeditor of four books on reading research, the author of more than thirty articles and book chapters, a set of resource materials on textbook adoption, and a review of the 1992 NAEP in Reading. With two colleagues, she wrote the Center's summary of Marilyn Adams's important book, *Beginning to Read: Thinking and Learning about Print*. Her most recent publication is *Literacy for All: Issues in Teaching and Learning*. Her research interests have included instructional materials, beginning reading, and textbook adoption procedures. She is presently serving as consultant to the Texas Education Agency for the Texas Reading Initiative.

INTRODUCTION

Background

Teaching all children to read and write is one of this nation's most important challenges. Our intention in writing *Reading Instruction and Assessment: Understanding the IRA Standards* is to help meet that challenge by explaining and elaborating the key standards for reading professionals developed by the International Reading Association (IRA), the major professional organization concerned with the promotion of literacy.

As one of its recent tasks, the IRA's 1997–1998 Standards and Ethics Committee (Daniel R. Hittleman, Chair) took on the challenge of writing standards for professionals involved in the teaching of reading. In 1998, the IRA published *Standards for Reading Professionals, Revised*, which replaced the 1992 version of the IRA's *Standards for Reading Professionals*. The current publication describes what reading professionals should know and be able to teach with regard to developing literacy. Although they are titled *Standards for Reading Professionals*, the *Standards* appear to us to be more broadly targeted for literacy and language arts professionals because they include writing as well as reading.

According to the committee that developed the *Standards*, the overall purpose of the document is to assist educational and governmental agencies to identify qualified personnel to deliver effective literacy programs. In so doing, the *Standards* are intended to: (1) help shape and evaluate programs of teacher preparation; (2) guide the assessment of the qualifications of literacy professionals; and (3) inform private and state agencies, policymakers, and the general public about literacy instruction.

The *Standards* are organized into three broad categories: Knowledge and Beliefs about Literacy, Instruction and Assessment, and Organizing and Enhancing a Reading Program. Each category is divided into competencies, which are one-sentence descriptions of what the literacy professional should know or be able to do. In recognition that different categories of reading professionals and paraprofessionals need different levels of understanding of the competencies, the *Standards* are also divided into three levels of proficiency: Awareness, Basic Understanding, and Comprehensive Understanding. (These categories of reading professionals and the levels of proficiency are defined in the *Standards for Reading Professionals, Revised*.)

In our view, the heart of the *Standards* is the category, Instruction and Assessment. This category includes six subcategories: Being able to (1) create an environment to foster literacy, (2) teach word identification, vocabulary, and spelling, (3) promote comprehension, (4) develop study strategies, (5) teach writing skills and strategies, and (6) assess student achievement. This Instruction and Assessment category consists of thirty competencies in these six subcategories. Table 1 lists the Instruction and Assessment competencies in each of the six subcategories.

TABLE 1   Instruction and Assessment Competencies of the *IRA Standards for Reading Professionals, Revised* (pp. 13–17)

5.0   CREATING A LITERATE ENVIRONMENT

The reading professional will be able to:

5.1   create a literate environment that fosters interest and growth in all aspects of literacy;

5.2   use texts and trade books to stimulate interest, promote reading growth, foster appreciation for the written word, and increase the motivation of learners to read widely and independently for information, pleasure, and personal growth;

5.3   model and discuss reading and writing as valuable, lifelong activities;

5.4   provide opportunities for learners to select from a variety of written materials, to read extended texts, and to read for many authentic purposes;

5.5   provide opportunities for creative and personal responses to literature, including storytelling;

5.6   promote the integration of language arts in all content areas;

5.7   use instructional and information technologies to support literacy learning; and

5.8   implement effective strategies to include parents as partners in the literacy development of their children.

6.0   WORD IDENTIFICATION, VOCABULARY, AND SPELLING

The reading professional will be able to:

6.1   teach students to monitor their own word identification through the use of syntactic, semantic, and graphophonemic relations;

6.2   use phonics to teach students to use their knowledge of letter/sound correspondence to identify sounds in the construction of meaning;

6.3   teach students to use context to identify and define unfamiliar words;

6.4   guide students to refine their spelling knowledge through reading and writing;

6.5   teach students to recognize and use various spelling patterns in the English language as an aid to word identification; and

6.6   employ effective techniques and strategies for the ongoing development of independent vocabulary acquisition

7.0   COMPREHENSION

The reading professional will be able to:

7.1   provide direct instruction and model when and how to use multiple comprehension strategies, including retelling;

7.2   model questioning strategies;

7.3   teach students to connect prior knowledge with new information;

7.4   teach students strategies for monitoring their own comprehension;

7.5   ensure that students can use various aspects of text to gain comprehension, including conventions of written English, text structure and genres, figurative language, and intertextual links; and

7.6   ensure that students gain understanding of the meaning and importance of the conventions of standard written English (e.g., punctuation or usage).

(continued)

TABLE 1 *(continued)*

8.0 STUDY STRATEGIES

The reading professional will be able to:

8.1 provide opportunities to locate and use a variety of print, nonprint, and electronic reference sources;

8.2 teach students to vary reading rate according to the purpose(s) and difficulty of the material;

8.3 teach students effective time-management strategies;

8.4 teach students strategies to organize and remember information; and

8.5 teach test-taking strategies.

9.0 WRITING

The reading professional will be able to:

9.1 teach students planning strategies most appropriate for particular kinds of writing;

9.2 teach students to draft, revise, and edit their writing; and

9.3 teach students the conventions of standard written English needed to edit their compositions.

10.0 ASSESSMENT

The reading professional will be able to:

10.1 develop and conduct assessments that involve multiple indicators of learner progress; and

10.2 administer and use information from norm-referenced tests, criterion-referenced tests, formal and informal inventories, constructed response measures, portfolio-based assessments, student self-evaluations, work/performance samples, observations, anecdotal records, journals, and other indicators of student progress to inform instruction and learning.

Purpose of *Reading Instruction and Assessment: Understanding the IRA Standards*

We believe that the Instruction and Assessment competencies need further explication in order to meet the purposes of the IRA document. The single-sentence competencies contain many terms that may be unfamiliar or unclear to some of the intended audiences of the *Standards*. Furthermore, the IRA document contains no statement of the theory or research that guided the development of the competencies.

The purpose of our book, *Reading Instruction and Assessment: Understanding the IRA Standards*, therefore, is to explain and discuss the 30 competencies contained in the Instruction and Assessment category of the IRA *Standards for Reading Professionals, Revised* for the intended audiences of the IRA *Standards*—teacher educators, preservice and inservice reading professionals and their administrators, employees of private and state agencies, policymakers, and the general public. *Reading Instruction and Assessment: Understanding the IRA Standards* is intended to supplement the *IRA Standards* in order to make them more accessible and useful. It is not intended as a comprehensive overview of the reading field, and it is not intended to serve as a reading methods textbook.

We provide an interpretation of each competency and, when available, a brief review of research related to the competency. In cases where research is not available, we draw upon conventional wisdom, good classroom practice, and common sense. In our discussion, we do not comment on the levels of proficiency specified in the IRA *Standards* because we believe that the analysis we provide will be useful for professionals at *all* the levels of proficiency.

At times, in our attempt to explain the IRA competencies, we are critical of them. Sometimes we found a competency to be unclear. Sometimes we were unable to identify a theoretical or research-based rationale for a competency. Sometimes a competency omitted what we believed to be critical content. In addition to identifying some problems with the competencies included in the IRA *Standards*, we also identified several research-based topics that the IRA *Standards* did not include as competencies. We discuss these in the final chapter.

Organization of *Reading Instruction and Assessment: Understanding the IRA Standards*

Reading Instruction and Assessment: Understanding the IRA Standards is divided into six sections, one for each of the six subcategories of Instruction and Assessment. Each chapter focuses on a single competency or a set of closely related competencies. (See Table 2 for a list of the competencies discussed in each chapter.) Beginning with the competency(ies) included in that chapter, each chapter is organized in the following sections:

1. *Interpretation.* This section includes our interpretation of the intention of the stated competency. If we found that the intention of the competency was not clear, we used our professional judgment to clarify the competency.

2. *Related Research.* This section includes a brief discussion of the major findings of research related to our interpretation of the competency, when such research was available. As previously mentioned, if research was not available, we drew on conventional wisdom, good classroom practice, and common sense.

3. *What Does This Mean for You, the Teacher?* This section discusses instructional implications following from the research, including mention of specific methods and references to other practical resources for reading professionals. This section is intended only to present the highlights of recommended practice for reading professionals; it is certainly not sufficient as the sole preparation for teaching that competency.

4. *Summary.* In this section we provide a summary of the research and instructional implications related to the competency.

5. *References.* In addition to references for cited works, we try to suggest references that will be helpful for the intended audiences of the IRA *Standards*. These recommended references are indicated with an asterisk.

Following the chapters discussing the Instruction and Assessment competencies, *Reading Instruction and Assessment: Understanding the IRA Standards* concludes with a chapter presenting our recommendations for revising the existing competencies or adding research-based competencies that we believe are crucial for reading professionals but that were overlooked in the current version of the IRA *Standards*.

Summary

The purpose of the IRA *Standards for Teaching Professionals, Revised* is to help educators meet the challenge of teaching all children to read and write. We hope that *Reading Instruction and Assessment: Understanding the IRA Standards* will serve that purpose by helping to clarify and extend the Instruction and Assessment category of the IRA *Standards*. We want to provide the audience of the *Standards* with a brief overview of some of the most useful information currently available about how to effectively teach reading and writing to all students in U.S. schools. In addition, we want to provide readers with suggestions of other areas they might consider in preparing and certifying reading professionals or in improving their own practice as reading professionals. We hope that, in some small way, *Reading Instruction and Assessment: Understanding the IRA Standards* will help teachers and other educators with their most important job—teaching all children to read and write.

Acknowledgments

We want to thank the following individuals for the time and work they put into reviewing drafts of this book; they provided many constructive comments and suggestions: Linda Lewis-White, Eastern Michigan University; Marian Jean Dreher, University of Maryland; Ann Hall, Southwest Texas State University; and Jean M. Casey, California State University, Long Beach.

TABLE 2   Instruction and Assessment Competencies by Chapter

Chapter No.	Chapter Title	Competencies from IRA *Standards*
1	Literate Environment	5.1, 5.2, 5.3, 5.4
2	Personal Response to Literature	5.5
3	Integrating Language Arts across Content Areas	5.6
4	Technology	5.7
5	Parent Involvement	5.8
6	Cueing Systems	6.1
7	Phonics	6.2
8	Context	6.3
9	Connecting Reading, Writing, and Spelling	6.4, 6.5
10	Vocabulary	6.6
11	Direct Instruction of Comprehension Strategies	7.1
12	Questioning Strategies	7.2
13	Prior Knowledge	7.3
14	Monitoring Comprehension	7.4
15	Aspects of Text	7.5, 7.6
16	Multiple Sources	8.1
17	Adjusting Reading Rate	8.2
18	Time-Management Strategies	8.3
19	Organizing and Remembering Information	8.4
20	Test-Taking Strategies	8.5
21	Writing Process	9.1, 9.2
22	Conventions of Written English	9.3
23	Assessment	10.1, 10.2

1 Literate Environment

COMPETENCY 5.1
Create a literate environment that fosters interest and growth in all aspects of literacy.

COMPETENCY 5.2
Use texts and trade books to stimulate interest, promote reading growth, foster appreciation for the written word, and increase the motivation of readers to read widely and independently for information, pleasure, and personal growth.

COMPETENCY 5.3
Model and discuss reading and writing as valuable, lifelong activities.

COMPETENCY 5.4
Provide opportunities for learners to select from a variety of written materials, to read extended texts, and to read for many authentic purposes.

Interpretation

These four competencies are the first of eight competencies in the subcategory of "Creating a Literate Environment." The phrase *literate environment* refers to a classroom, school, or home in which literacy is fostered and nurtured. The intent of these four competencies is that reading professionals should know how to establish conditions that will stimulate interest and growth in the language arts.

The most general statement of the intent of this category is Competency 5.1: Create a literate environment that fosters interest and growth in all aspects of literacy. Competencies 5.2–5.8 are elaborations of Competency 5.1. We have chosen to group Competencies 5.2, 5.3, and 5.4 with Competency 5.1 because they are closely related to each other and to the core components of the literate environment referred to in Competency 5.1. Competencies 5.2 and 5.4 both refer to the need to encourage wide reading from a variety of texts for a variety of purposes.

Related Research

Based on knowledge of how literacy develops, experts have identified a number of conditions that should foster and nurture the development of literacy in the school and classroom. These components of a literate environment are described below.

Models

Crucial to a literate environment are people who model an interest and involvement in literacy. Students need to see many examples of how readers and writers work and how reading and writing are used for various purposes. All children, but especially those children who do not have rich literacy experiences at home, benefit from interacting with skilled readers and writers who value reading and writing and who openly share the pleasure and satisfaction that reading and writing bring to them. These models may be teachers, other adults from the school or community, or older students. This component of a literate environment is reflected in Competency 5.3: Model and discuss reading and writing as valuable, lifelong activities.

Materials

A second component of a literate environment is the materials available to support literacy. It is especially important that classrooms include a large number of books and other reading materials. As Competencies 5.2 and 5.4 suggest, students should read lots of books and other materials over sustained periods of time for authentic purposes. "Some of the best 'practice' for enhancing reading skill occurs when students are given greater opportunity to read everyday materials" (Pearson, 1993, p. 508).

Amount, or volume, of reading is related to many positive cognitive consequences (Cunningham & Stanovich, 1998; National Reading Panel, 2000), including reading comprehension (Anderson, Wilson, & Fielding, 1988; Pressley, 2000); vocabulary knowledge (Herman, Anderson, Pearson, & Nagy, 1987; Pressley, 2000); ability to monitor comprehension (Pinnell, 1989); disposition to read independently (Ingram, 1982); and English grammar skills (Elley & Mangubhai, 1983). In addition, a consistent positive relationship exists between amount of voluntary reading and gains on standardized reading achievement tests (Pearson & Fielding, 1991).

In response to research showing positive effects of volume of reading, many teachers have established blocks of structured reading time daily. These periods are usually called SSR (Sustained Silent Reading), USSR (Uninterrupted Sustained Silent Reading), DEAR (Drop Everything and Read), or SQUIRT (Super Quiet Reading Time). Such programs are advocated in most reading methods textbooks for prospective elementary teachers and have become very popular in U.S. classrooms. Research, however, has not supported programs to encourage more reading (National Reading Panel, 2000). As the National Reading Panel concludes,

> There are few beliefs more widely held than that teachers should encourage students to engage in voluntary reading and that if they did this successfully, better reading

achievement would result. Unfortunately, research has not clearly demonstrated this relationship. In fact, the handful of experimental studies in which this idea has been tried raise serious questions about the efficacy of some of these procedures (pp. 3–27).

Besides a variety of reading materials, a literate environment will contain materials to encourage and facilitate writing. Paper, dry erase boards, pencils, pens, crayons, and markers should be readily available, as should materials for students to make their own books. Finally, a literate environment will include computers with high quality reading and writing software, integrated media technology, and access to the Internet (Sharp, Bransford, Goldman, Kinzer, & Soraci, 1992).

Physical Setting

The third component of a literate environment is the physical setting—the arrangement of the classroom in a manner that strongly supports literacy. To support extended reading, books need to be readily available to children in classroom, school, and public libraries. Access to books through libraries has a positive relationship to reading achievement (Krashen, 1993, 1995). Because classroom libraries provide the most immediate access to books, they are likely to increase the amount of voluntary reading students do both in and out of school (Fractor, Woodruff, Martinez, & Teale, 1993). The availability of good classroom and school libraries is especially important to low-income or at-risk students because they typically have less access to reading materials outside of school (Braunger & Lewis, 1997).

In addition to ready access to books and other materials, a literate environment will encourage writing in a writing center where children work independently or in small groups on writing projects. An area for computers is a requirement of a literate classroom environment. Finally, a literate environment for younger children will also include a listening center (where children can listen to recordings of books read by fluent readers) and a drama center (where, for example, children can dramatize texts they are reading or listening to).

Atmosphere

A final component of a literate environment is the atmosphere created in the school and classroom. The ambience of a literate environment conveys a strong message that reading and writing are valued. In a literate environment, the teacher reads aloud to students daily. Students are given plenty of time to read independently, with a partner, or in a group. Time is set aside for students to share with each other what they have learned from reading and their personal responses to what they have read. Time is also provided for writing and for sharing writing. The sharing of reading and writing can involve cooperative and collaborative work in groups. Such group work has been shown to increase both achievement and productivity (Johnson & Johnson, 1987; Slavin, 1990).

In addition, a literate environment may include schoolwide efforts to encourage literacy, such as establishing reading incentive programs, setting aside a regular period for sustained silent reading throughout the school, scheduling "read alouds" by parents and community leaders, and inviting authors to visit the school.

In summary, a literate school or classroom environment has four key components: people who model an interest and involvement in literacy, materials that promote and facilitate student involvement in reading and writing, a physical setting that supports literacy, and an atmosphere pervaded by enthusiasm for and support of literacy.

What Does This Mean for You, the Teacher?

Basic guidelines for creating a literate environment were given in the preceding description of the four components of a literate environment. The guidelines will be elaborated here.

1. Model an interest and involvement in literacy. Show your students that you are a reader and a writer, that you value reading and writing, and that reading and writing bring lifelong pleasure and fulfillment. Share with them what you are reading and writing outside of the classroom. Read to your students with enthusiasm and expression. When they are engaged in silent sustained reading, you should read as well, to reinforce the idea that you value reading. In the same spirit, you should write to your students, for example, send them individual messages and write responses to their journal entries. When your students are writing, you, too, should write.

2. Provide materials that promote and facilitate reading and writing. Your classroom should contain a large number and variety of reading materials, including library books, personal books, magazines, newspapers, brochures, instructions, menus, transportation schedules, and other environmental print. Make sure there are materials that will both entertain and inform your students. If you are a teacher of beginning readers, your library should include "lots of easy stuff to read" (Allington & Cunningham, 1996). Try to obtain books that meet the interests of your students and reflect their cultural, linguistic, and social backgrounds. You can supplement the classroom library with temporary collections of library books related to particular topics or themes you are teaching.

Writing materials include paper, dry erase boards, pencils, pens, crayons, and markers, as well as materials for students to make their own books. If you teach younger children who cannot yet hold pencils well, you should provide manipulable letters (for example, magnetic letters or letters made of foam rubber). If you have a listening center, you will need audiotapes and the corresponding hard copies of a variety of text selections. If you have a drama center, you should include costumes, props, and, perhaps, materials for making puppets.

3. Create a physical setting that supports literacy. First and foremost, work on developing an extensive classroom library/reading center with a comfortable, inviting area for children to read. Cover your classroom walls with print of many kinds—covers or reviews of books, lists of rules and procedures, signs, charts, and the children's own written work. For beginning readers, it is helpful to also post labels with the names of objects. You should have an area for computers in your classroom. If you are teaching younger students, you will want to consider additional designated areas. For example, you may have a separate writing area, with tables where your students can work on their writing and readily accessible writing materials. You may also have a listening area, equipped with tape players and earphones. Finally, you may have an area for drama, perhaps including a puppet theater.

4. Create an atmosphere that fosters literacy. Read aloud to your students daily, and invite others (for example, parents, principals, other community members) to read to them as well. Read with enthusiasm and expression. Engage your students in the text by asking thought-provoking questions.

A few years ago, we might have suggested that you schedule at least one block of structured reading time daily, such as SSR, USSR, DEAR, or SQUIRT. Given the conclusions of the National Reading Panel cited earlier, however, we can no longer recommend such a procedure until research has revealed the conditions under which encouraging more reading in the classroom might produce gains in reading achievement.

You might encourage reading *outside* the classroom, however, by developing a book bag program. Book bags contain reading materials that students can take home to read with their families. Book-bag programs usually include opportunities for families to document what their children read and to respond in some way to the reading.

Support writing as well as reading. Provide time for writing for a variety of purposes and audiences; set aside time for sharing writing as well (see Chapter 21). Make sure that some of the students' writing is shared with families, perhaps by sending their writing home in the book bag or by inviting students to include a written response to a book in the book bag.

Participate in or initiate literacy activities that extend beyond your classroom, for example, schoolwide reading incentive programs, invitations to community leaders to read to your students, invitations to authors to visit the school, or writing competitions for students. Also try to provide an opportunity for your students to acquire library cards and to become familiar with the local public library.

Summary

A literate environment is the foundation for fostering and nurturing literacy. Competencies 5.1–5.4 pertain to establishing the critical components of a literate environment. These components are: people who model an interest and involvement in literacy, materials that promote and facilitate student involvement in reading and writing, a physical setting that supports literacy, and an atmosphere pervaded by enthusiasm for and support of literacy. Recommendations were offered for how reading professionals can establish a literate environment in the classroom.

REFERENCES

*Recommended for teachers

*Allington, R., & Cunningham, P. (1996). *Schools that work: Where all children read and write.* New York: Harper Collins.

*Anderson, R., Hiebert, E., Schott, J., & Wilkinson, I. (1985). *Becoming a nation of readers: The report on the commission on reading.* Champaign, IL: University of Illinois, Center for the Study of Reading.

Anderson, R., Wilson, P., & Fielding, L. (1988). Growth in reading and how children spend their time outside of school. *Reading Research Quarterly, 23,* 285–303.

Braunger, J., & Lewis, J. P. (1997). *Building a knowledge base in reading.* Portland, OR: Northeast Regional Educational Laboratory.

*Cunningham, A. E., & Stanovich, K. E. (1998). What reading does for the mind. *American Educator, 22*(1&2), 8–15.

Elley, W., & Mangubhai, F. (1983). The impact of reading on second language learning. *Reading Research Quarterly, 19,* 53–67.

*Fractor, J., Woodruff, M., Martinez, M., & Teale, W. (1993). Let's not miss opportunities to promote voluntary reading: Classroom libraries in the elementary school. *The Reading Teacher, 46,* 476–484.

Herman, P. A., Anderson, R. C., Pearson, P. D., & Nagy W. (1987). Incidental acquisition of word meanings from expositions with varied text features. *Reading Research Quarterly, 22,* 263–284.

Ingham, J. (1982). *Books and reading development: The Bradford book flood experiment.* 2nd ed. Exeter, NH: Heinemann Educational Books.

Johnson, D. W., & Johnson, R. T. (1987). *Learning together and alone: Cooperative, competitive, and individualistic learning.* 2nd ed. Englewood Cliffs, NJ: Prentice-Hall.

Krashen, S. (1993). *The power of reading.* Englewood, CO: Libraries Unlimited.

Krashen, S. (1995). *Every person a reader: An alternative to the California Task Force report on reading.* Culver City, CA: Language Education Associates.

National Reading Panel. (2000). *Teaching children to read: An evidence-based assessment of the scientific research literature on reading and its implications for reading instruction.* Washington, DC: U.S. Department of Health and Human Services.

Pearson, P. D. (1993). Teaching and learning reading: A research perspective. *Language Arts, 70*(6), 502–511.

Pearson, P. D. (1996). Foreword. In E. McIntyre & M. Pressley (Eds.), *Balanced instruction: Strategies and skills in whole language.* Norwood, MA: Christopher-Gordon.

Pearson, P. D., & Fielding, L. (1991). Comprehension instruction. In R. Barr, M. Kamil, P. Mosenthal, & P. D. Pearson (Eds.), *Handbook of reading research*, Vol. 2 (pp. 815–860). New York: Longman.

Pinnell, G. (1989). Success for at-risk children in a program that combines reading and writing. In J. Mason (Ed.), *Reading and writing connections.* Boston, MA: Allyn & Bacon.

Pressley, M. (2000). What should comprehension instruction be the instruction of? In M. L. Kamil, P. B. Mosenthal, P. D. Pearson, & R. Barr (Eds.), *Handbook of reading research*, Vol. III (pp. 545–561). Mahwah, NJ: Lawrence Erlbaum.

Sharp, D. L. M., Bransford, N. V., Goldman, S. R., Kinzer, C., & Soraci, S., Jr. (1992). Literacy in an age of integrated-media. In M. J. Dreher, & W. H. Slater (Eds.), *Elementary school literacy: Critical issues* (pp. 183–210). Norwood, MA: Christopher-Gordon.

Slavin, R. (1990). *Cooperative learning: Theory, research, and practice.* Englewood Cliffs, NJ: Prentice-Hall.

2 Personal Response to Literature

COMPETENCY 5.5
Provide opportunities for creative and personal responses to literature, including storytelling.

Interpretation

Competency 5.5 advocates providing opportunities for students to make creative and personal responses to literature (including storytelling), which is commonly referred to as "reader response." Reader response describes the unique interaction between the reader and the text within a particular reading context. Reader response approaches to literature encourage expression of independent thoughts, personal reflections, and emotional engagement both during and after a reading event. Readers can respond to a text in many ways, usually by writing and discussing, but also through drama, art, music, dance, and other forms of creative expression.

Related Research

The reader response approach to literature has been greatly influenced by the work of Louise Rosenblatt (1978, 1995). According to Rosenblatt, reading is a transaction between the reader and the text in which the reader's interpretation reflects both the meaning intended by the author and the meaning constructed by the reader. Meaning does not reside in a text, but is made by the reader. Therefore, different readers will have different interpretations of a text.

The nature of the transaction between reader and text depends on the stance or approach the reader takes to the text. Rosenblatt identifies two stances: the efferent and the aesthetic. In efferent reading, the reader's purpose is primarily focused on acquiring information or learning something new, that is, in taking something away from the text after reading. In contrast, a reader engaged in aesthetic reading is primarily concerned with the experience of living through the text. The reader does this by focusing on feelings, thoughts, enjoyment, and appreciation during reading. In aesthetic reading, the reader is "responding from the heart or the creative mind" (Sebesta, 1997, p. 546). Most reading is not exclusively efferent or exclusively aesthetic, but rather falls somewhere along an efferent–aesthetic continuum. Reader response approaches to literature, however, usually emphasize the aesthetic stance (Spiegel, 1998).

While Rosenblatt's transactional theory of reader response focuses on the elements of reader and text, other reader response theorists emphasize the importance of the context of the reader (e.g., Galda, 1988). In reader response theory, context refers to the many different communities to which the reader belongs, including both the broad, sociocultural community and the local or situational community, such as the classroom (Galda, 1988; Hancock, 2000). The various communities to which readers belong are assumed to influence their responses to texts.

In classrooms, reader response approaches take many forms, but they all contain two essential elements—reading and responding (Spiegel, 1998). In reader response approaches, an emphasis is placed on the students' reading a great deal of self-selected authentic literature, usually in silent reading periods in which students read at their own pace. Most approaches to reader response involve students writing personal responses to what they read, often in some form of journal. Another popular form of response is discussion (Spiegel, 1998). Often, discussion follows a personal written response. Many different kinds of literature discussion groups have been developed, but they share the purpose of eliciting personal responses from students and making these public through discussion (Graves, Juel, & Graves, 1998). (See the section *What Does This Mean for You, the Teacher?* for a discussion of some of these kinds of discussion groups.) Besides written and oral responses, other forms of reader response can include the expressive arts: drama, art, music, and dance (Hancock, 2000).

Reader response theory has spawned a number of research studies during the past thirty-five years, including research on the benefits of the implementation of reader response approaches to literature in elementary and middle school classrooms. Research has found the following benefits to reader response approaches (Spiegel, 1998):

1. **Growth in ownership of and responsibility for reading and responding.** Students who participate in response-based activities assume more responsibility for reading, running discussion groups, and explaining their interpretations.
2. **Increased personal connections with literature.** With reader response approaches, students tend to make more personal connections between literature, their own lives, and the world.
3. **Greater appreciation for multiple interpretations.** Students in response-based classrooms develop an appreciation and tolerance for different interpretations and tend to be more open to new ideas.
4. **Growth in critical reading and thinking.** Students who participate in reader response approaches become more reflective and more critical readers who engage in higher levels of thinking and construct richer understandings of what they read.

5. Increased repertoire of responses. Through reader response approaches, students acquire a variety of responses that they can then use with new literature.
6. Growth as strategic readers. Students in response-based classrooms grow in several ways as readers. They tend to perceive themselves as successful, confident readers. They become more aware of the strategies they use as readers, and more responsible for monitoring and "fixing up" their own comprehension. Participants in reader response approaches develop a good understanding of the elements of literature. They learn to clarify their ideas, develop speed and fluency, and become more effective listeners. Finally, several studies have shown that students who participate in reader response approaches perform better on standardized achievement tests than students in more teacher- and text-dominated classrooms or classrooms in which the tested skills were specifically taught.

In summary, reader response approaches, based primarily on Rosenblatt's transactional theory of reader response, emphasize the interaction of reader, text, and context in the reader's unique construction of the meaning of what is read. Two key elements of reader response approaches are extensive *reading* of self-selected authentic literature and *responding* through writing, discussion, and the expressive arts.

What Does This Mean for You, the Teacher?

Your students' responses to literature will be fostered in a classroom environment in which you model an interest and involvement in literacy, provide plenty of opportunity to read a variety of genres, styles, and authors, and provide time and encouragement for responding to literature in a variety of ways (see Chapter 1). This section continues with a more detailed explanation of the different forms of reader response to literature: written response, oral response, and the expressive arts.

Written Response to Literature

Most reader response approaches involve students responding to literature in writing, usually in some form of journal. Journals provide for informal writing experiences that encourage personal reflection and growth.

If your students need assistance in learning how to write responses to text, you can provide them with teacher-constructed question prompts. The prompts should be open-ended and should encourage students to construct meaning based on personal interaction with the text. These prompts should also elicit higher order thinking. Some examples of question prompts are: How does this story relate to your own life? What advice would you give Character X at this point in the story? Do you believe Character X made the right choice? Why?

As students become familiar with responding in writing, they will require fewer prompts and gain more independence. At this point, you may wish to use any of several different kinds of journals. In a *literature response journal*, you encourage your students to record their thoughts as they occur during reading, rather than retrospectively after reading. A *dialogue journal* is an ongoing written conversation between the student and you (although it could be another person) about the book being read. In a *character journal*, your students assume the identity of one of the story's characters and engage in first-person interaction with the story. In a *double-entry journal*, your students divide the journal page in half lengthwise. On the left they record direct quotes, events, or other information from the text, and on the right they record their responses to each of these entries.

Journals may be shared with you the teacher, as well as shared in discussion groups, exchanged with peers for comment, and used as the basis for further writing experiences. Your students' journals will provide you with valuable information about their development as readers. Regardless of which journal type you use, you should respond to your students' journal writing on a regular basis for the purpose of exchanging ideas and thoughts and encouraging further response.

Oral Response to Literature

A second common way to respond to literature is orally. The most popular form of oral response to literature is discussion in literature response groups. The purpose of literature response groups is to allow students to exchange thoughts and feelings, refine ideas, and think creatively and critically about the topics, ideas, and issues they have read about. Many variations of literature response groups have been developed over the past few years, including Literature Circles (Daniels, 1994), Grand Conversations (Wells, 1995), Book Clubs (McMahon, Raphael, Goatley, & Pardo, 1997), and literature discussion groups (Routman, 1991). These variations of discussion groups share the following common elements: (1) They consist of a small group of students (usually four to seven) who have read the same piece of literature (usually selected by the students, but may be assigned by the teacher); (2) the discussion is led by students; the teacher may participate as a group member; (3) students are encouraged to contribute their personal responses and listen to one another's responses.

Response to Literature through the Expressive Arts

Drama, Dance, Art, and Music.   Although frequently reserved for enrichment activities, the expressive arts—drama, dance, art, and music—offer immense possibilities for personal response to literature. Inviting response through the arts can help you address the needs of all types of learners. In addition, by allowing your students the freedom to explore and choose a variety of response modes, you are encouraging the development of lifelong readers and learners.

In the area of drama, your students can respond to literature through pantomime, improvisation, story dramatization, readers' theater, puppetry, and original plays. (See McCaslin,1996 for more ideas on drama.) For some of your students, dance is a powerful means of self-expression and a vehicle for constructing meaning from literature. Art is another important medium for extending response to literature. Many children can more readily share personal response through drawing than they can through oral or written language. In fact, according to the *Standards for the English Language Arts* (1996), jointly published by the IRA and the National Council of Teachers of English (NCTE), visual representation is now generally accepted as one of the language arts. Musical response to literature may include singing songs or selecting a musical background for a drama presentation or other form of response. (For more ideas on responding to literature through the expressive arts, see Cecil & Lauritzen, 1994 and Hancock, 2000.)

Summary

Competency 5.5 recommends providing opportunities for students' personal responses to literature. Based primarily on the reader response theory of Louise Rosenblatt, reader response approaches emphasize each reader's unique interpretation of a text. Research has established several benefits of responding to literature. Personal response can take several forms. While writing and discussion are the most common forms of response, students can also respond through drama, dance, art, and music.

REFERENCES

*Recommended for teachers
*Atwell, N. (1987). *In the middle: Writing reading, and learning with adolescents*. Portsmouth, NH: Heinemann.
*Cecil, N. L., & Lauritzen, P. (1994). *Literacy and the arts for the integrated classroom: Alternate ways of knowing*. New York: Longman.
*Daniels, H. (1994). *Literature circles: Voice and choice in the student-centered classroom*. York, ME: Stenhouse.
Galda, L. (1988). Readers, texts and contexts: A response-based view of literature in the classroom. *The New Advocate, 1*(2), 82–102.
*Graves, M. F., Juel, C., & Graves, B. B. (1998). *Teaching reading in the 21st century*. Boston, MA: Allyn & Bacon.
*Hancock, M. R. (2000). *A celebration of literature and response: Children, books, and teachers in K-8 classrooms*. Upper Saddle River, NJ: Merrill.
*McCaslin, N. (1996). *Creative drama in the classroom and beyond*. 6th ed. White Plains, NY: Longman.
*McMahon, S. I., Raphael, T. E., Goatley, V. J., & Pardo, L. S. (1997). *The Book Club connection: Literacy learning and classroom talk*. Newark, DE: International Reading Association and New York: Teachers College Press.
National Council of Teachers of English and International Reading Association. (1996). *Standards for the English language arts*. Urbana, IL and Newark, DE: Author.
Rosenblatt, L. M. (1978). *The reader, the text, the poem: The transactional theory of the literary work*. Carbondale, IL: Southern Illinois University Press.
Rosenblatt, L. M. (1995). *Literature as exploration*. 5th ed. New York: Appleton-Century-Crofts.

*Routman, R. (1991). *Invitations: Changing as teachers and learners K–12*. Portsmouth, NH: Heinemann.

*Sebesta, S. L. (1997). Having my say. *The Reading Teacher, 50*(7), 542–549.

*Spiegel, D. L. (1998). Reader response approaches and the growth of readers. *Language Arts. 76*(1), 41–48.

*Wells, D. (1995). Leading grand conversations. In N. L. Roser & M. G. Martinez (Eds.), *Book talk and beyond: Children and teachers respond to literature* (pp. 132–139). Newark, DE: International Reading Association.

3 Integrating Language Arts across Content Areas

COMPETENCY 5.6
Promote the integration of language arts in all content areas.

Interpretation

This competency encourages teachers to integrate the language arts into content area subjects such as social studies, science, math, and the arts—in other words, to embed literacy instruction throughout the curriculum.

Although the term *integration* is rather ambiguous (Gavelek, Raphael, Biondo, & Wang, 1999; Pearson, 1994), we believe the intent of the competency is that teachers should use the language arts as "functional tools rather than curricular entities to be studied or mastered in their own right" (Pearson, 1994, p. 19). In other words, teachers should encourage students to use the language arts as tools or means for learning in the content areas. In this way, the language arts are not seen as isolated skills but as tools to be used in authentic learning activities (McGinley & Tierney, 1989). The content areas thus provide learning contexts in which the language arts are used for a purpose.

In the competency, "language arts" probably refers to the six language arts that were described in the IRA/NCTE *Standards for the English Language Arts*. These six language arts include the four traditional language arts—reading, writing, speaking, listening—as well as two additional language arts, viewing and visually representing.

Different approaches that have emphasized integrating the language arts in the content areas include content area reading, writing across the curriculum, whole language, inquiry-based learning, project methods, and thematic units. At the elementary level, at least, a popular attempt to integrate curricula, including the language arts, is through thematic instruction, or thematic units (Shanahan, 1997). This chapter will discuss various possibilities for integrating the language arts in the content areas.

Related Research

Proponents of integrated instruction (Gavelek, Raphael, Biondo, & Wang, 1999; Lipson, Valencia, Wixson, & Peters, 1993; Shanahan, 1997; Shanahan, Robinson, & Schneider, 1995) claim several advantages of integration:

1. Greater initial learning: Students will learn more and have a deeper grasp of the ideas studied;
2. Greater probability of transfer: Students will perceive greater authenticity and meaningfulness to their learning and will thus be able to apply it more readily to real problems;
3. Greater motivation: Because students find learning more meaningful, they will enjoy it more and be more committed to further learning;
4. Greater efficiency: Because integration is a more efficient way to learn, there is more instructional time to cover more curriculum.

Despite strong claims and enthusiasm for integrated instruction, little research exists to support it. As Shanahan put it, "Surprisingly, given the long history and nearly universal acceptance of the idea of integration at all levels of education, there have been few empirical investigations of its effects" (1997, p. 133). A more recent review found "few data-driven studies on integrated instruction of any sort . . ." (Gavelek, Raphael, Biondo, & Wange,1999, p. i), including the integration of language arts with other content areas (Morrow, Pressley, Smith, & Smith, 1997).

The few available studies on the integration of language arts with other content areas, however, offer promising results. Most research on the integration of the language arts has been done with science content. Studies done at the third (Morrow, Pressley, Smith, & Smith, 1997), fourth (Romance & Vitale, 1992), and fourth- and fifth-grade levels (Bristor, 1994) have shown that integrated reading and science programs can enhance student achievement in both reading and science, improve student attitudes toward learning, and improve instructional efficiency by eliminating the need for separate instruction in reading (Romance & Vitale, 1992). Similarly, the Explorer's program, a six-week summer program for upper elementary students that integrates language arts and science, has been shown to foster learning in both language arts and science (Bruning & Schweiger, 1997).

One particularly notable effort to integrate language arts and science instruction is the Concept-Oriented Reading Instruction (CORI) program (Guthrie, Van Meter, Hancock, Alao, Anderson, & McCann, 1998; Guthrie, Van Meter, McCann, Wigfield, Bennett, Poundstone, Rice, Faibisch, Hunt, & Mitchell, 1996). CORI is a year-long instructional intervention designed to increase students' engagement (the motivated use of conceptual knowledge and strategies) in reading, writing, and science. Research conducted in third- and fifth-grade classrooms found that, compared to traditional instruction using a basal reader and science textbook, students who received CORI instruction were more likely to learn and use cognitive strategies for comprehending multiple texts, and, by learning strategies, were more adept at learning science concepts and applying their knowledge to novel situations (Guthrie et al., 1998).

Some research has also investigated integrating the language arts with social studies. Smith and his colleagues (Smith, 1993; Smith, Monson, & Dobson, 1992) found that using trade books (books available through libraries and bookstores) to supplement a study of U.S. history greatly enhanced elementary students' learning of historical concepts. Similarly, Guzzetti, Kowalinski, and McGowan (1992) found that sixth graders learned more about China when reading both trade books and a textbook than when reading only a textbook.

Another research-based approach to integrating the language arts with the content areas is "Questioning the Author" (QtA) (Beck, McKeown, Hamilton, & Kucan, 1997). In QtA, students and the teacher work collaboratively to understand content area textbooks (although the method can also be applied to narratives). A key feature of QtA is that students grapple with meaning while they are reading instead of discussing questions after they have finished reading. The teacher initiates and sustains discussion during reading through the use of carefully designed "queries," or probes that focus on meaning, and "discussion moves," which are actions the teacher takes to keep students involved in constructing a meaningful interpretation of the text. When applied over extended periods of time, QtA has been successful at improving elementary students' comprehension and comprehension monitoring.

Another area of relevant research concerns the use of trade books in the curriculum. Most of the studies cited above used trade books as the sole or major source of reading. A number of other studies have demonstrated that experiences with literature in the classroom promote interest in reading, language development, reading achievement, and growth in writing ability (Galda & Cullinan, 1991; Morrow, 1992; Morrow, O'Connor, & Smith, 1990). Although these studies did not examine the effect of literature on learning content, they did demonstrate a positive effect on learning language arts.

What Does This Mean for You, the Teacher?

Competency 5.6 encourages you to help your students use the language arts as tools or means for learning in the content areas. Fortunately, there are many opportunities for you to accomplish this goal. We will first consider how you can incorporate the individual language arts in content area instruction; then we will discuss thematic units as a possibility for integrating language arts and content learning.

First, consider reading. One of the easiest and most popular ways to integrate reading into all content areas is to use trade books, or children's literature, as a source from which students learn the content. Trade books, including nonfiction as well as other genres (see Chapter 16), can increase students' conceptual knowledge as well as motivate and sustain their interest. Trade books appropriate for all content areas are readily accessible. Many useful resources are available to help you find appropriate trade books. For example, libraries contain several reference books that can assist you in locating children's literature related to particular topics; the American Library

Association publishes magazines such as *Book Links: Connecting Books, Libraries, and Classrooms*, which provides annotated bibliographies of children's literature related to particular topics as well as other features useful to classroom teachers; many textbooks on children's literature can provide guidance on selecting appropriate literature; and a large number of children's literature resources are available on the World Wide Web.

You can also incorporate many different types of writing into your content area instruction. For example, your students may take notes during a science experiment; they may make journal entries about a book they are reading; they may write letters soliciting information from community members or thanking them for a guest appearance; they may write word problems in mathematics and explanations of how they solved problems; they may write research reports; or they may compose stories or poetry using concepts they have learned. One of the most popular forms of writing in classrooms is journals. See Chapter 2 for several examples of journals that can be used in response to reading materials or other learning experiences in the content areas.

The content areas afford many opportunities for you to integrate oral literacy—speaking and listening—into the curriculum. Discussion, such as the QtA method presented in the section on "Related Research," is one common way to promote oral literacy. Another form of discussion is literature response groups, particularly if you are using children's literature as a source from which students are learning the content. (See Chapter 2 for a discussion of literature response groups.) Other ways to promote oral literacy include dramatic activities such as role-playing, dramatizations of historical events, scripts for radio or television shows, and reader's theater. In reader's theater, participants read and interpret scripts adapted from literature, including nonfiction (Young & Vardell, 1993).

The content areas also provide many opportunities for you to include the language arts of viewing and visually representing, or visual learning. Of course, much learning in the content areas already involves visual learning—observing phenomena in science, studying artifacts and maps in social studies, and examining shapes, patterns, and figures in mathematics. Textbooks and trade books typically include lavish graphic aids, including illustrations, diagrams, and photographs. Computers provide many opportunities for visual learning, through the Internet, which is teeming with graphics, pictures, photographs, maps, and other visuals, and through CD-ROMS, which, for example, allow children access to the great museums of the world. Of course, even without computers you can introduce art in the form of reproductions of paintings, sculptures, and photographs related to the curriculum. (See, for example, Cecil & Lauritzen, 1994; Pappas, Kiefer, & Levstik, 1995.)

You can also encourage students to represent information visually. Students can represent information in the content areas through drawings, graphs and charts, posters, graphic organizers, models, and dioramas. They can take photographs, make videotapes and films, and create graphics on the computer. They can write and illustrate class books, newspapers, and magazines that reflect their learning in the content areas.

Of course, you should also remember the importance of teaching your students to visualize, or form mental images, of the content they are learning about. Visualization has been shown to be an effective comprehension strategy (see Chapter 12).

So far in this section we have suggested ways in which you can integrate each of the six language arts into the content areas. Another possibility, and a very popular one these days, is to integrate the curriculum through the use of thematic units. In thematic units, students engage in inquiry into a basic thematic idea chosen either by the teacher or students. Examples of themes are "The Environment" or "Human Journeys." By organizing teaching around themes or topics, it is possible to integrate the language arts in meaningful ways across mathematics, social studies, science, and the arts. Thematic units offer the possibility of using the language arts methods described above in a coherent and meaningful way. Although the use of thematic units is intuitively appealing, thematic teaching can be difficult, for example, choosing appropriate themes, making sure that no content area is shortchanged, respecting the social and cultural domains of the disciplines, and ensuring the inclusion of direct instruction (Shanahan, et al., 1995; Shanahan, 1997). Fortunately, there are several helpful guides to thematic teaching available (e.g., Pappas, Kiefer, & Levstik, 1999).

Summary

Competency 5.6 encourages reading professionals to promote the integration of the language arts—reading, writing, speaking, listening, viewing, and visually representing—into all content areas. In this way, the language arts become tools for learning. Although there is relatively little research on integrated curricula, the existing research shows a positive effect of integration on both learning and attitude toward learning. Suggestions for incorporating each of the language arts were offered. In addition, the possibility of using thematic units to integrate the language arts with the content areas was introduced.

REFERENCES

*Recommended for teachers

*Beck, I. L., McKeown, M. G., Hamilton, R. L., & Kucan, L. (1997). *Questioning the Author: An approach for enhancing student engagement with text*. Newark, DE: International Reading Association.

Bristor, V. J. (1994). Combining reading and writing with science to enhance content area achievement and attitudes. *Reading Horizons, 35*(1), 30–43.

Bruning, R., & Schweiger, B. M. (1997). Integrating science and literacy experiences to motivate learning. In J. T. Guthrie & A. Wigfield (Eds.), *Reading engagement: Motivating readers through integrated instruction* (pp. 149–167). Newark, DE: International Reading Association.

Cecil, N. L., & Lauritzen, P. (1994). *Literacy and the arts for the integrated classroom: Alternative ways of knowing*. New York: Longman.

Galda, L., & Cullinan, B. E. (1991). Literature for literacy: What research says about the benefits of using trade books in the classroom. In J. Flood, J. M. Jensen, D. Lapp, & J. R. Squire (Eds.), *Handbook of research on teaching the English language arts* (pp. 529–535). New York: Macmillan.

Gavelek, J. R., Raphael, T. E., Biondo, S. M., & Wang, D. (1999). *Integrated literacy instruction: A review of the literature.* Ann Arbor, MI: University of Michigan, Center for the Improvement of Early Reading Achievement, CIERA Report #2-001.

Guthrie, J. T., Van Meter, P., Hancock, G. R., Alao, S., Anderson, E., & McCann, A. (1998). Does Concept-Oriented Reading Instruction increase strategy use and conceptual learning from text? *Journal of Educational Psychology, 90*(2), 261–272.

Guthrie, J. T., Van Meter, P., McCann, A. D., Wigfield, A., Bennett, L., Poundstone, C. C., Rice, M. E., Faibisch, F. M., Hunt, B., & Mitchell, A. M. (1996). Growth of literacy engagement: Changes in motivations and strategies during concept-oriented reading instruction. *Reading Research Quarterly, 31*(3), 306–332.

Guzetti, B. J., Kowalinski, B. J., & McGowan, T. (1992). Using a literature-based approach to teaching social studies. *Journal of Reading, 36*(2), 114–122.

International Reading Association and National Council of Teachers of English. (1996). *Standards for the English language arts.* Urbana, IL: Author.

*Lipson, M. Y., Valencia, S. W., Wixson, K. K., & Peters, C. W. (1993). Integration and thematic teaching: Integration to improve teaching and learning. *Language Arts, 70,* 252–263.

McGinley, W., & Tierney, R. J. (1989). Traversing the topical landscape: Reading and writing as ways of knowing. *Written Communication, 6,* 243–269.

Morrow, L. M. (1992). The impact of a literature-based program on literacy achievement, use of literature, and attitudes of children from minority backgrounds. *Reading Research Quarterly, 27*(3), 251–275.

Morrow, L. M., O'Connor, E., & Smith, J. (1990). Effects of a story reading program on the literacy development of at risk kindergarten children. *Journal of Reading Behavior, 22,* 255–275.

Morrow, L. M., Pressley, M., Smith, J. K., & Smith, M. (1997). The effect of a literature-based program integrated into literacy and science instruction with children from diverse backgrounds. *Reading Research Quarterly, 32*(1), 54–76.

*Pappas, C. C., Kiefer, B. Z., & Levstik, L. S. (1999). *An integrated language perspective in the elementary school: An action approach.* 3rd ed. White Plains, NY: Longman.

Pearson, P. D. (1994). Integrated language arts: Sources of controversy and seeds of consensus. In L. M. Morrow, J. K. Smith, & L. C. Wilkinson (Eds.), *Integrated language arts: Controversy to consensus* (pp. 11–31). Boston, MA: Allyn & Bacon.

Romance, N. R., & Vitale, M. R. (1992). A curriculum strategy that expands time for in-depth elementary science instruction by using science-based reading strategies: Effects of a year-long study in grade four. *Journal of Research in Science Teaching, 29*(6), 545–554.

*Shanahan, T. (1997). Reading–writing relationships, thematic units, inquiry learning . . . in pursuit of effective integrated literacy instruction. *The Reading Teacher, 51*(1), 12–19.

*Shanahan, T., Robinson, B., & Schneider, M. (1995). Avoiding some of the pitfalls of thematic units. *The Reading Teacher, 48*(8), 718–719.

Smith, J. A. (1993). Content learning: A third reason for using literature in teaching reading. *Reading Research and Instruction, 32*(3), 64–71.

Smith, J. A., Monson, J. A., & Dobson, D. (1992). A case study on integrating history and reading instruction through literature. *Social Education, 56*(7), 370–375.

Young, T., & Vardell, S. (1993). Weaving Reader's Theater and nonfiction into the curriculum. *The Reading Teacher, 46,* 396–405.

4 Technology

COMPETENCY 5.7
Use instructional and information technologies to support literacy learning.

Interpretation

This competency recognizes that technology holds great promise for increasing access to information as well as acquiring and using literacy. Technology is an integral part of literacy instruction today in many classrooms and will become even more so in the future.

Some ways in which technology is being used to support reading include (Leu, 2000):

1. Instructional software. Instructional software, including multimedia software, presents instructional programs focused on reading.
2. Networked information environments, such as the Internet. The "information superhighway," including E-mail, provides many opportunities for accessing and using written text in the classroom (e.g., Garner & Gillingham, 1996; Garner & Gillingham, 1998; Leu & Leu, 1998)
3. Electronic or "talking" books. Electronic books are hypermedia texts with speech support and, sometimes, illustrations. If beginning readers follow along in the text, they may learn to read some words while practicing listening comprehension.
4. "Responsive texts" and "supportive texts." These electronic texts are designed to facilitate comprehension and learning by providing various kinds of support to the reader, for example, providing definitions for unknown words.

Technology can also support writing, especially with word-processing programs. Because of the close match between word-processing and process writing approaches (see Chapter 21), "computer technology is the quintessential tool for process writing" (Leu, 2000, p. 773). Desktop publishing and multimedia authoring software programs allow students to publish their writing using integrated text and graphics, as well as different text styles and formats.

Finally, the literacy learning of special populations can be enhanced through the use of various "assistive" technologies. For example, visually impaired students can use computers that increase the size of text, provide Braille displays, or incorporate audio descriptions. For students with hearing impairments, computers can help integrate text, sign, and speech. Computers with speech synthesizers that pronounce words as they are being typed into a word-processing program may help some students. Multimedia programs that integrate text, speech, and visual aids can assist the literacy development of second-language learners.

Related Research

In this section we will briefly discuss two areas of research related to computers and literacy. The first area of research concerns the effect of informational and instructional technologies on literacy learning. Recent reviews of technology and literacy learning (Kamil, Intrator, & Kim, 2000; Leu, 2000; National Reading Panel, 2000) lament the fact that research has not kept pace with developments in computer technology that have the potential to support literacy. The National Reading Panel concluded that "It is extremely difficult to make specific instructional conclusions based on the small sample of experimental research available" (2000, p. 6-2). For example, in the area of writing, word-processing programs have been commercially available since 1979 (Pea & Kurland, 1987). Yet, although numerous studies have been conducted, "we cannot reach an overall simple conclusion concerning such questions as: Does using computers improve writing?" (Hartley, 1991, p. 369). Research on writing with computers has at least revealed that the use of computers promotes interaction and collaboration (Kamil, Intrator, & Kim, 2000).

Despite the lack of research, the National Reading Panel did offer the following five tentative conclusions for educators (National Reading Panel, 2000, pp. 6-8–6-9):

1. Computers can be used for some reading instructional tasks, for example, with some instructional software and because of the increased opportunities for students to interact with text.

2. Word processing is a helpful addition to reading instruction, not only because reading and writing are related cognitive processes, but also because word-processing programs facilitate the drafting, revising, and editing phases of process writing.

3. Multimedia computer software can be used for reading instruction (although there is little research on how, when, and for whom literacy learning with multimedia occurs).

4. Computers have a motivational use in reading instruction. Working with computers can increase students' motivation, interest, enjoyment, task involvement, persistence, time on task, and school retention.

5. Hypertext has a great deal of potential in reading instruction. Despite the dearth of research, hypertext, particularly in conjunction with the use of the Internet, is being used in many classrooms.

The second related body of research we discuss here focuses on the availability and use of computers in classrooms, and includes some challenges facing the use of technology to support literacy. There are varying reports on the availability and use of computers in classrooms. According to *Education Week*'s 1999 *National Survey of Teachers' Use of Digital Content*, with responses from 1,407 elementary, middle, and high school teachers, computer technology is in about 80 percent of the nation's classrooms; over half of classrooms are connected to the World Wide Web; and schools have an average of one instructional computer for every 5.7 students (Fatemi, 1999).

Even though the number of computers in classrooms has been steadily increasing, many teachers feel they still do not have enough computers. Another survey found that 75 percent of teachers who do not use software for instruction cite a lack of classroom computers as a reason (Trotter, 1999). More than one third of teachers who responded to this survey have no computers for instructional use in their classrooms, while another 40 percent have only one or two computers. Indeed, "most experts do agree that access to technology still creates barriers for too many schools" (Jerald & Orlofsky, 1999).

An issue related to the accessibility of computers in classrooms is the variable accessibility students have to computers in their homes, usually due to the socioeconomic status of the family. (Eighty percent of students in families with an income of $75,000 or more use a computer at home, compared with only 20 percent of students in families with an income of less than $30,000 a year [Jerald & Orlofsky, 1999].) As a result of the varying availability of computers in the home, teachers are faced with considerable variation in the technological skills that students bring to the classroom.

Even when teachers have electronic resources available in the classroom, they often do not use them to their full potential. In the *Education Week* survey, only 53 percent of teachers reported using instructional software in their classrooms, while 61 percent reported using the Web for instructional purposes (Fatemi, 1999). Among the major reasons teachers report for not making greater use of digital resources are lack of training, lack of time, expense of the software, and difficulty finding appropriate, quality content (Fatemi, 1999).

"Professional development is the essential ingredient to making the most of digital content in the classroom" (Trotter, 1999), yet most teachers feel ill-prepared for the digital age. The Federal Office of Technology Assessment found that a majority of teachers felt inadequately trained to use computer technologies (Office of Technology Assessment, 1995). According to a 1998 survey by the National Center for Education Statistics, only about one in five teachers felt "very well prepared" to integrate education technology in the grade or subject they taught (Trotter, 1999). Unfortunately, "too many teachers still lack the training and confidence to infuse computers into their teaching" (Jerald & Orlofsky, 1999).

A second reason teachers fail to use instructional and information technologies to their full potential is lack of time. Teachers need time to attend technology courses and workshops, to experiment with the new technologies, to plan lessons using digital content, to integrate that content into the curriculum, and to share their experiences with other teachers. In addition to out-of-classroom time, teachers are also concerned about the amount of in-classroom time it takes to implement instructional and information technologies. In the *Education Week* survey, about half of the teachers who use software for instruction found that both the "amount of preparation time necessary" and "amount of class time necessary" were big or moderate problems in using software (Fatemi, 1999).

A third reason for teachers not making greater use of digital resources is the expense of software. Teachers responding to the *Education Week* survey cited "expense" as the biggest barrier to making greater use of software, with 82 percent claiming it as a big or moderate problem (Fatemi, 1999).

The difficulty of finding appropriate software with quality content is a fourth reason that teachers do not make greater use of digital resources. Market forces—the pressure to produce for the game and play markets rather than for the educational markets—appear to strongly affect the quality of instructional software. "Good educational software and teacher-supported tools, developed with a full understanding of principles of learning, have not yet become the norm" (Bransford, Brown, & Cocking, 1999, p. 218). Another researcher concluded, "there's been very little research to help educators identify high-quality software" (Zehr, 1999, p. 4). The Internet also poses challenges. Teachers need to learn how to determine whether the information on a site is valid, and they have to figure out how to let students explore the Web without encountering inappropriate material (Zehr, 1999).

In addition to concerns about the quality of digital content, teachers are also concerned about whether digital resources satisfy curriculum requirements, particularly in states with academic standards and high-stakes testing. "The problem is that many teachers don't know where to go to select software titles and Web sites to fit their curriculum needs" (Hoff, 1999, p. 51).

In summary, although instructional and informational technology offer a great deal of promise, little research-based guidance is currently available to teachers. Furthermore, teachers also encounter significant challenges in implementing technology effectively in their classrooms.

What Does This Mean for You, the Teacher?

We agree with Labbo, Reinking, and McKenna (1999) that "digital forms of reading and writing not only can be but must be integrated into the mainstream of literacy instruction . . ." (p. 323). In this section, we first discuss some of the more common and accessible digital resources. Second, we offer some thoughts regarding the challenges facing classroom teachers who are using digital resources in the classroom.

Word Processors

We agree with the Reading Panel that word processing is a helpful addition to reading instruction, not only because reading and writing are related cognitive processes, but also because word processing facilitates drafting, revising, and editing. We encourage you to take full advantage of word processing by integrating it into all phases of the writing process rather than just having students use the computer to type their final draft. By having students keep an electronic file for their writing, you reinforce the idea that writing is never a final product, but awaits further modification (Labbo, Reinking, & McKenna, 1999).

In addition, if you have the resources available, you will want your students to learn to use *desktop publishing* programs, which allow them to combine text and graphics, and to create professional-looking publications, either for print or on the Web. Or, you may teach your students to use *multimedia* and *presentation tools*, which enable them to turn their research and written text into interactive or animated presentations, with sophisticated art and sound effects.

The Internet

The Internet provides both the World Wide Web and E-mail. The World Wide Web, with its mixture of text, graphics, sound, and images, allows students to navigate to various Web sites. Through the Web, students are able to use search engines to locate information on virtually any topic, and then jump to related topics. They can pose questions to experts and other students, and they can publish their research reports. Students can also engage in Internet projects, which are collaborative learning projects designed within the framework of a thematic or topical unit.

As their teacher, you need to ensure that your students develop some expertise at navigating (also known as "browsing" or "surfing") the Web in order to find information efficiently and effectively. You may need to provide activities, such as guided tours with "bookmarks," that take them directly to the sites you want them to visit. You also need to ensure that they do not access inappropriate sites.

With the Internet, your students can also use E-mail to engage in instantaneous written conversation with students and teachers throughout the world. For example, through key pal correspondence, the electronic equivalent of pen pals, students can exercise their literacy skills while they learn about other students, schools, and cultures. Students and teachers can also join E-mail discussion groups by subscribing to a mailing list or listserv.

With both word processing and the Internet, you should try to take advantage of opportunities to foster students' social or collaborative learning experiences. For example, you can strategically pair students who are more and less knowledgeable about the technology so that the less knowledgeable student can internalize successful strategies (Labbo, Reinking, & McKenna, 1999).

Software Programs

Many basal reading programs now include accompanying software to supplement their instruction. In addition, other publishers have inundated the market with innovative packages that often include highly interactive multimedia CD-ROM software. One example of educational software, often available on CD-ROM, is electronic books. Presented to readers on the monitor, electronic text uses the conventions of traditional books, such as pages, tables of content, and indices. Some electronic books are informational, providing in-depth information about a particular topic; others are engagingly interactive stories.

Assistive Technologies

As discussed in the first section of this chapter, there are many technologies available to assist students with special needs. Depending on your students' needs and developmental level, you will want to become informed about, and make use of, available assistive technologies. Additional information on using technology to support the literacy learning of special populations of learners is available in Labbo, Reinking, and McKenna (1999).

Other Audio and Audiovisual Technology

Although you are most likely to think of computer technologies in relationship to Competency 5.7, other technologies can support literacy learning. For example, audio versions of books have been available for some time. Students can benefit from hearing books read engagingly and fluently. Finally, high-quality videocassettes and films are also available for a wide variety of children's books. These resources may motivate students to read or provide the basis for writing activities.

We caution, however, that audio and audiovisual technology should not be a substitute for reading. In other words, students who have difficulty reading should not simply be sent to the listening center to listen to books instead of reading them. As discussed in Chapter 1, and mentioned throughout this book, volume or amount of reading is strongly related to success in reading. In incorporating instructional and information technology in your teaching, do not lose sight of the importance of wide reading!

Although you may have many opportunities to use computers in your classroom, you also face many challenges, as suggested in the "Related Research" section. One challenge is accessibility. Although computers are more available in classrooms than ever before, you still may not have computers in your classroom, or enough computers, to use effectively for instruction. Furthermore, even if computers are available, you may not have access to the Internet.

A related challenge is the variable accessibility your students have to computers at home. Obviously, students who have access to computers in the home are likely to be much more technologically sophisticated than students who come from homes without computers. Because the presence of computers in the home is so tied to socioeconomic status, it is especially important to ensure that the "digital divide" (Jerald & Orlofsky, 1999) is not perpetuated or exacerbated in your classroom. In other words, you need to provide students without home computers with instruction and opportunities so that they can "catch up" to their more technologically advanced peers.

One of your greatest challenges in implementing instructional and information technology may be your own lack of training. As noted, many teachers feel underprepared to use, much less teach students how to use, much of the available digital resources. Mastering basic technology skills is only part of the challenge. Teachers also need to learn how to use technology effectively in instruction, for example, how to integrate technology into the existing curriculum.

To assist in preparing teachers to use technology, the International Society for Technology in Education (ISTE) is engaged in an ongoing process of developing standards regarding what teachers should know about and be able to do with technology. These standards are beginning to guide teacher preparation programs. In the meantime, you will want to take advantage of any existing opportunities to enhance your knowledge of instructional issues related to technology, such as workshops, conferences, and courses. In addition, you may need to request additional in-service training in your district.

Lack of time, of course, is always an issue for classroom teachers. You need time to learn about technology yourself; you need time to plan lessons, projects, and units that integrate digital resources effectively; you need classroom time for students to complete those lessons, projects, and units; and you need time to evaluate their work. Although we have no solution to this problem, we are confident that the more you know about instructional and information technology, the more efficiently you will be able to use it to accomplish your goals.

Expense is another challenge for which we can offer no solution. Fortunately, if you have an Internet connection, you are probably able to use the World Wide Web and E-mail free of charge. Software programs and CD-ROMs, however, are generally not free. In some cases, however, educational discounts are available to teachers.

Given that software is expensive, you will want to purchase the highest quality software available. We mentioned the issue of software quality in the section on "Related Research." Fortunately, many excellent reviews of software are available. For example, the International Society for Technology in Education (ISTE) publishes software reviews in their monthly journal, *Learning and Leading with Technology*. The Association for Supervision and Curriculum Development publishes an annual software review. The International Reading Association also publishes program reviews in its professional journals and newsletters.

Summary

Competency 5.7 urges teachers to use instructional and informational technology to support literacy learning. Indeed, technology is a part of the literacy instruction in many schools today and will become even more so in the future. Nevertheless, this competency is more challenging for teachers to implement than many of the other IRA competencies. In addition to the lack of research-based guidelines, teachers face issues of accessibility of hardware and software, inadequate training, time constraints, expense, and the difficulty of finding appropriate, high-quality electronic resources.

REFERENCES

*Recommended for teachers

Bransford, J. C., Brown, A. L., & Cocking, R. R. (Eds.). (1999). *How people learn: Brain, mind, experience, and school*. Washington, DC: National Academy Press.

Fatemi, E. (1999). Building the digital curriculum. *Education Week, 19*(4), 5–8.

*Garner, R., & Gillingham, M. G. (1996). *Internet communication in six classrooms: Conversations across time, space, and culture*. Mahwah, NJ: Lawrence Erlbaum.

Garner, R., & Gillingham, M. (1998). The internet in the classroom: Is it the end of transmission-oriented pedagogy? In D. Reinking, L. D. Labbo, M. McKenna, & R. Kieffer (Eds.), *Literacy for the 21st century: Technological transformations in a post-typographic world* (pp. 221–231). Mahwah, NJ: Lawrence Erlbaum.

Hartley, J. (1991). Psychology, writing and computers: A review of research. *Visible Language, 25*(4), 338–375.

Hoff, D. J. (1999). Digital content and the curriculum. *Education Week, 19*(4), 51–57.

Jerald, C. D., & Orlofsky, G. F. (1999). Raising the bar on school technology. *Education Week, 19*(4), 58–62.

Kamil, M. L., Intrator, S. M., & Kim, H. S. (2000). The effects of other technologies on literacy and literacy learning. In M. L. Kamil, P. B. Mosenthal, P. D. Pearson, & R. Barr (Eds.), *Handbook of reading research*, Vol. III (pp. 771–788). Mahwah, NJ: Lawrence Erlbaum.

*Labbo, L. D., Reinking, D., & McKenna, M. C. (1999). The use of technology in literacy programs. In L. B. Gambrell, L. M. Morrow, S. B. Neuman, & M. Pressley (Eds.), *Best practices in literacy instruction* (pp. 311–327). New York: Guilford.

Leu, D. J., Jr. (2000). Literacy and technology: Deictic consequences for literacy education in an information age. In M. L. Kamil, P. B. Mosenthal, P. D. Pearson, & R. Barr (Eds.), *Handbook of reading research*, Vol. III (pp. 743–770). Mahwah, NJ: Lawrence Erlbaum.

*Leu, D. J., Jr., & Leu, D. D. (1998). *Teaching with the Internet: Lessons from the classroom* (2nd ed.). Norwood, MA: Christopher-Gordon.

National Reading Panel. (2000). *Teaching children to read: An evidence-based assessment of the scientific research literature on reading and its implications for reading instruction*. Washington, DC: U.S. Department of Health and Human Services.

Office of Technology Assessment. (1995). *Teachers & technology: Making the connection*. Washington, DC: U.S. Government Printing Office.

Pea, R. D. & Kurland, D. M. (1987). Cognitive technologies for writing. In E. Z. Rothkopf (Ed.), *Review of research in education*, Vol. 14 (pp. 277–326). Washington, DC: American Educational Research Association.

Trotter, A. (1999). Preparing teachers for the digital age. *Education Week, 19*(4), 37–43.

Zehr, M. A. (1999). Screening for the best. *Education Week, 19*(4), 13–22.

5 Parent Involvement

COMPETENCY 5.8
Implement effective strategies to include parents as partners in the literacy development of their children.

Interpretation

This competency recognizes the crucial role of the family, especially parents, in the development of literacy. Experts agree that school success begins at home and that parents are the first and most important people in the education of their children. The intent of Competency 5.8 is for reading professionals to encourage and assist parents to become effective partners in helping their children acquire literacy. Note that, although we use the term *parents* in this chapter, because that is the term used in the IRA competency, it is probably more appropriate, with today's changing family composition, to say "the parent, parents, or primary caregiver(s)."

Related Research

Research conducted with diverse populations of students shows that "parent involvement in almost any form appears to produce measurable gains in student achievement" (Henderson, 1988, p. 150). What is true of academic achievement in general is certainly also true of achievement in reading and writing. Research has established a strong relationship between the home environment and children's acquisition of school-based literacy. Children who are successful in reading and writing at school tend to come from homes having the following characteristics (Anderson, Hiebert, Scott, & Wilkinson, 1985; Braunger & Lewis, 1997; Morrow, 1995; Snow, Burns, & Griffin, 1998):

1. Literacy is valued. Parents are enthusiastic readers and writers. They model an interest in and enjoyment of reading a variety of texts, such as books, newspapers, magazines, and manuals. Parents also write—grocery lists, notes, letters, E-mail messages, and so forth.

2. Plenty of print materials are readily available. Children have easy access to a large number and variety of children's literature, as well as other reading and writing materials. Parents take their children regularly to the public library, help them acquire a library card, and encourage them to check out books.

3. Academic achievement is encouraged. Parents value education and expect their children to learn to read and write in school. Parents encourage and monitor their children's interest and achievement in language and literacy.

4. Parents frequently read to and with children. Parents read large numbers of books to preschoolers. When their children begin to read, parents listen to their oral reading, providing assistance as needed.

5. Parents provide a language-rich environment in which they interact verbally with their children. Parents engage their children in conversations about experiences and activities in general and about books in particular. Parents ask questions about books they or their children are reading aloud. These questions encourage thinking and help their children relate the story to real-life events. Parents answer their children's questions fully and expansively. Elaborated answers help their children acquire general world knowledge and knowledge of language, including vocabulary.

6. Parents continue to be personally involved with their children's academic growth in school, including their development as readers and writers. Parents show an interest in their children's learning and achievement in school. Parents do their best to facilitate their children's continuing growth and success as readers and writers.

It is important to understand that, even though these characteristics tend to be correlated with success in reading and writing in school, no direct cause–effect relationship between these characteristics and school success has been established. Many children who do not enjoy the advantages associated with these characteristics still become successful readers and writers.

What Does This Mean for You, the Teacher?

You can do much to include parents as partners in the literacy development of their children. It is important, however, for you to acknowledge, respect, and accommodate socially, culturally, and linguistically diverse families. You must not assume that a student who seems to lack in school-based literacy comes from a family that does not value or practice literacy. For example, the family may own few books, yet enjoy a rich oral tradition of storytelling (Morrow, 1995). It is also important to remember that parents with limited English proficiency may be very willing, but unable to follow some of your suggestions. For example, if parents cannot read English, they will not be able to read newsletters you send home, nor will they be able to read books in English to or with their child.

Finally, it is important to recognize that including parents as partners in the literacy development of their children is not a one-way relationship in which the only valid and reliable advice is transmitted from teachers to parents. For example, parents may provide valuable information on culture-specific literacy forms (for example, telling folktales) that is helpful to you in teaching their child. Parents can visit your classroom and share literacy forms and experiences from their own culture or language. We hope you will keep these points in mind as we offer the following recommendations about how you can involve parents in their children's literacy development.

One major way in which you can encourage the involvement of parents is by communicating with them about literacy instruction in your classroom. Keep parents informed. Most parents want to understand the goals and purposes of your instruction, your expectations for their children, your evaluation procedures, and their children's progress throughout the school year. Parent–teacher conferences and school "open houses" are common ways to introduce this information at the beginning of the school year. You can sustain the communication throughout the school year, however, in some of the following ways:

1. Invite parents into your classroom as observers, as guest speakers, and as volunteers. Parents may wish to simply observe your teaching methods, content, and style. Parents can also serve as guest speakers, for example, to tell stories, read books, share hobbies and describe vocations, and to explain cultural traditions. You may also invite parents to volunteer in your classroom. Parent volunteers can, for example, listen to children read aloud, confer with children during Writer's Workshop, help children publish their books, and work on special projects.

2. Send home letters, newsletters, and student work. For example, when you are introducing a new unit or project, tell parents your goals and expectations, inform them how they can help at home, and encourage them to contact you if they have questions or concerns. Send parents examples of their children's work, explaining the assignment and what it shows about their children's progress and achievement. You can also encourage your students to write to their parents, explaining what they are learning in school and including self-selected samples of their work.

3. Call parents. Occasionally, you may want to telephone parents to converse about their children's achievement. Too frequently, teachers only call parents when there is a problem, but phone calls can be used to convey good or neutral news as well.

A second major way you can promote parent participation is by encouraging their involvement in their children's literacy activities at home. Many of the following suggestions stem from research on characteristics of homes of children who succeed in school-based literacy, as discussed in the section on "Related Research." Other helpful suggestions can be found in Morrow (1995) and on the National Parent Information Network Web site: http://www.npin.org (a project of the ERIC system that is administered by the National Library of Education in the U.S. Department of Education).

1. Elicit parent support for reading. Because reading achievement is directly related to the amount of reading children do, it is important to elicit parent support for reading at home. Encourage parents to read to and with their children, and to talk about the books they are reading, perhaps during a specially designated family reading time. Urge parents to encourage their children to pursue independent or voluntary reading as well. Encourage parents to help their children obtain library cards and make regular use of public and school libraries.

2. Provide parents with methods and materials to use at home. For example, you can send home book bags containing books at the student's reading level, writing supplies, and instructions or suggestions for what students and their parents can do with the materials. (See also Chapter 1.) A recent government program available on the U.S. Department of Education's Web site is designed to send home a reading activity each day to help parents support what their children are learning at school (International Reading Association, 1999).

3. Help build bridges between home and school literacy (Braunger & Lewis, 1997). Because the types and forms of literacy practiced in some homes can be different from school-based literacy, it is important to be aware of the differences and to seek opportunities to draw on the parents' and children's social, cultural, and linguistic strengths. For example, an assignment involving interviewing older relatives about events in their lives might be well suited for a family with a strong oral tradition. Sending home literature from the family's culture in a book bag might help forge a connection. And, as previously mentioned, you can invite parents into your classroom to share their language and their literacy traditions.

Summary

In summary, you can include parents as partners in the literacy development of their children in two major ways—by keeping them informed about literacy instruction in your classroom and by encouraging and assisting their involvement in their children's literacy development. In so doing, you should be sensitive to possible social, cultural, and linguistic differences between the home literacy of your students and the literacy expectations of school.

REFERENCES

*Recommended for teachers

Anderson, R., Hiebert, E., Scott, J., & Wilkinson, I. (1985). *Becoming a nation of readers: The report on the commission on reading*. Champaign, IL: University of Illinois, Center for the Study of Reading.

Braunger, J., & Lewis, J. P. (1997). *Building a knowledge base in reading*. Portland, OR: Northwest Regional Educational Laboratory.

*Henderson, A. T. (1988). Parents are a school's best friend. *Phi Delta Kappan*, (Oct.), 149–153.
*International Reading Association. (1999). Focus on family involvement. *Reading Today*, *17*(1), 3–4.
*Morrow, L. M. (1995). Family literacy: New perspectives, new practices. In L. M. Morrow (Ed.), *Family literacy: Connections in schools and communities* (pp. 5–10). Newark, DE: International Reading Association.
Snow, C. E., Burns, M. S., & Griffin, P. (Eds.). (1998). *Preventing reading difficulties in young children*. Washington, DC: National Academy Press.

CHAPTER

6

Cueing Systems

COMPETENCY 6.1
Teach students to monitor their own word identification through the use of syntactic, semantic, and graphophonemic relations

Interpretation

This standard proposes that reading professionals help students learn to monitor their identification of printed words by taking advantage of three sources of information:

1. Syntactic information is the grammatical structure of the sentences in which the words appear. The first-grade girl who sees "The girl is playing in the sand" and reads it as "The girl is sand playing" is not taking advantage of the grammatical structure of the spoken English she knows so well.

2. Semantic information is the meaning of the sentences as well as the passage in which the words appear. The first-grade boy who sees "The girl is playing in the sand" and reads it as "The girl is playing in the soap" is trying to use the beginning sound of *sand* to read the word, but is not paying much attention to the meaning of the word he produces.

3. Graphophonic information is the sound–symbol and sound–spelling pattern relationships of which the words are composed. The student who reads "The girl is playing in the dirt" is attending to the meaning of the sentence, but is not paying sufficient attention to the spelling of *sand*.

The three sources of information (syntactic, semantic, and graphophonic) listed in Competency 6.1 are often combined and labeled "the three cueing systems." Descriptions of these cueing systems are found in many discussions of beginning reading instruction and appear in many materials used in staff development workshops. These descriptions are often accompanied by a graphic display consisting of three interlocking circles of equal size. For example, in one graphic display, the three circles are titled *Structure (Syntactic Cue System)*, *Meaning (Semantic Cue System)*, and *Visual (Graphophonic Cue System)*.

These graphic displays frequently include a related question in each of the circles for teachers to pose to their students. To help students access the syntactic cueing system, teachers are to ask, "Does it sound right?" To help students access the semantic cueing system, teachers are to ask, "Does it make sense?" And to help students access the graphophonic cueing system, teachers are to ask, "Does it look right?"

Related Research

In the past decade, a number of reading theorists have cited the importance of helping young students learn to attend to the information inherent in each of the three cueing systems, particularly when they encounter words that they have trouble identifying. The emphasis placed on these three sources of information centers on the importance of students understanding that reading is a meaning-getting process, not one of merely "calling out" words in print.

Goodman (1986) asserts that three language systems interact in written language: the graphophonic (sound and letter patterns), the syntactic (sentence patterns), and the semantic (meanings). He proposes that these three systems must work together and cannot be isolated for instruction. Goodman emphasizes that students need to read whole texts (not single words and isolated sentences) so as to have the opportunity to draw on the three cueing systems as they read.

Clay (1988) writes about these same three sources of information as only some of many sources of information that readers use as they read. But she specifically discusses young readers' uses of meaning, structure, and visual information by embedding these concepts in three categories of other reading strategies she considers important to reading: (1) strategies that maintain fluency, (2) strategies that detect and correct error, and (3) strategies for "problem-solving" new words. She proposes that each of these strategies involves students engaging in a network of *cues* that are provided by the meaning of the story or passage (semantic), its language structure (syntactic), and the visual information of the print (graphphonic). Clay (1988) points out that what is of the greatest importance is how young readers access and use the information provided by this network of cues.

Others have developed many variations and modifications of the ideas associated with the three cueing system. Heilman, Blair, and Rupley (1998) present a somewhat different view of the cueing systems of written language. They list whole-word recognition, phonics, structure, and context. Their discussion of syntactic and semantic *clues* (rather than *cues*) occurs in the section of their book labeled *contextual analysis*. They do not include the use of graphophonic clues in this discussion but devote a separate section to sight vocabulary, phonics, and structural analysis. The importance they place on teachers giving careful attention to helping their students develop useful graphophonic knowledge is apparent when they advise that "Students can use contextual clues only when they can recognize or sound out most of the words in a sentence" (Heilman, Blair, & Rupley, 1998, p. 192).

Durkin (1998) also describes semantic cues and syntactic cues as contextual cues. She defines contextual cues as "prompts that derive from known words" (p. 163). She, too, points to the importance of young readers learning to pay attention to graphophonic cues as well as those cues deriving from context. She argues that contextual cues can be useful to students when they encounter unknown words but that their knowledge of graphophonic cues must be used to restrict the possibilities. For example, the blank in this sentence (representing the word a student cannot read) could be filled with any number of words: "At the park, the boys had fun on the _____." But if the student attends to the beginning letter of the troublesome word, the possibilities are more restricted: "At the park, the boys had fun on the s_____." On the other hand, if the student pays attention to the two letters at the beginning and the three-letter ending of the troublesome word, "At the park, the boys had fun on the sw—ing, the possibilities are almost totally restricted, and it is highly likely that the student will correctly identify the word as *swing*.

It is the amount of emphasis given to each of these three sources of information, and the point in the sequence of beginning reading instruction at which they are emphasized, that are a concern of still other reading educators. In a chapter tracing the history of the development of the three cueing systems, Adams (1998) states her concerns: "the three-cueing schematic is sometimes presented as a rationale for subordinating the value of the graphophonemic information to syntax and semantics and, by extension, for minimizing and even eschewing attention to the teaching, learning, and use of the graphophonemic system" (p. 79). She further warns that "such marginalization of the role of spelling to speech correspondences is alarmingly discrepant with what research has taught us about the knowledge and processes involved in learning to read."(p. 79). She contends that scientific research demonstrates that students who become good readers depend on their understanding of and use of spellings and spelling–sound correspondences. Adams also contends that poorly developed knowledge or facility with spellings and spelling–sound correspondences is the most pervasive cause of reading delay or disability.

Finally, it is important to note that, although the *Report of the National Reading Panel* (2000) does not include any discussion of the three cueing systems, it does provide a great deal of research evidence for the importance of including phonics instruction in kindergarten and first-grade classrooms. The goal of phonics instruction is to help children better understand and utilize the information contained in the graphophonemic cueing system.

What Does This Mean for You, the Teacher?

How can you best deal with these often conflicting points of view about when and how to help students learn to use graphophonic, semantic, and syntactic sources of information to identify words? In considering these ideas about the sources of information that young readers can use to identify words, it is important to remember that the disagreements are not about the usefulness of any one of them. Rather, the disagreements center on when they should be emphasized in a program of beginning reading instruction and at what point in the process of identifying words students should be encouraged to focus on one or more than one of these sources of information. Specifically, how can you help your students take advantage of these sources of information, when, and for what purposes?

Durkin (1998) calls for you to maintain *balance* as you help your students learn to use both context (semantic and syntactic) and graphophonic cues when attempting to read words that are visually unfamiliar to them. In particular, she urges you to keep in mind that reading is a sense-making process as you help your students learn to ask two questions when they encounter unknown words. First, "What word would make sense here?" Then, after selecting a possible word, "Does *this* word make sense here?

Durkin emphasizes the importance of teaching your students graphophonic information and how to use it while reading. She points out that when students' well-developed graphophonic knowledge is combined with their use of contextual cues, the result is that the time it takes to recognize words is reduced. In making this observation, she points to the positive relationship between speed of word recognition and comprehension, and the negative relationship between slow word recognition and comprehension: "The more time spent on a word, the more likely will the pause interfere with comprehension" (Durkin, 1998, p. 179).

Graves, Juel, and Graves (1998) suggest that you emphasize different sources of information at different times as your students develop as readers. They advocate that you encourage your beginning readers to use what they know about language, the world, the context of the story, and the accompanying illustrations to support their not very well-developed skill in word identification. But they also urge that you give direct attention to simultaneously developing your students' graphophonemic word-identification skill, and for some very important reasons. They point out, as that children learn how specific letters relate to sounds, these cues to word identification should take precedence over contextual and picture cues, because letter–sound cues provide much more reliable information and a more effective means to word identification than do contextual cues or illustrations.

Adams (1990) points out the fundamental importance of your students learning to use graphophonemic information to sound out words. She says such knowledge will provide your students with a means of deciphering written words that are visually unfamiliar. In acknowledging that your students can learn to identify the complete spellings of a number of individual words visually—without sounding them out—Adams points out that students cannot learn *enough* words by learning one whole word at a time to independently read all of the words they encounter in even first- and second-grade texts. In contrast, when your students have useful knowledge of letter–sound relationships and know how to apply this knowledge, "they can sound out an unfamiliar word, discovering or confirming its identity all by themselves" (p. 89).

Adams gives two reasons for her advice to teach children not to use contextual cues as the primary means of identifying words that are visually unfamiliar: (1) Contextual cues are an unreliable source for word identification because the meaning of a passage so often depends on its less familiar words, the very words that your students are least likely to know; (2) overreliance on contextual cues will not encourage your students to study the spellings of visually unfamiliar words so as to increase their familiarity with those words. "Thus," she says, ". . . if a student uses context to guess right on one occasion, she or he may be no better prepared to identify the word on the next" (p. 89).

Like Durkin, Adams urges you to help your students learn to combine contextual support with useful knowledge of letter–sound correspondences. She suggests that, when your students encounter a word that is hard for them to read, you encourage them to take time to study it. They should reflect on its spelling, then consider its meaning using the information available from context. Finally, after they have "worked over" the new word, they should return to the beginning of the sentence to which it belongs and reread the sentence. As their teacher, you can certainly model and prompt your students to learn how to work on words that are unfamiliar.

In concluding her argument in support of the importance of helping children learn graphophonemic relationships and spelling patterns, Adams observes that context plays an important role in determining the meaning, rather than the identity, of unknown words. She advises you to provide your students with specific instruction in the strategic use of context, but cautions that "Good readers decode rapidly and automatically. Younger and poor readers tend to rely on context, partly because they do not have sufficient knowledge of spelling patterns to rely on instead" (1990, p. 92). And she warns that problems with basic decoding skills "may be the most common, and can be the most serious source of reading difficulties" (1990, p. 92).

In contrast, a much-read writer of several teacher-oriented books, Routman (1994, p. 200b), emphasizes semantic and syntactic information in a list of cues written for parents who are helping their children with reading. Routman advises that, "To produce independent readers who monitor and correct themselves as they read, the following prompts are recommended *before* saying 'sound it out.'" Here is her list of advice:

Give your child a "wait time" of five to ten seconds. See what he or she attempts to do to help him- or herself.

"What would make sense there?"

"What do you think that would, could be?"

"Go back to the beginning and try that again."

"Skip over it and read to the end of the sentence (or paragraph). Now what do you think it is?"

"Put in a word that would make sense there."

"You read that word before on another page. See if you can find it."

"Look at how that word begins. Start it out and keep reading."

Tell your child the word.

This advice differs considerably from that of Durkin, Adams, and Graves, Juel, and Graves. In an attempt to put all of this information into its own useful context, we offer the advice of the Committee on the Prevention of Reading Difficulties in Young Children. As part of their "Recommendations for Practice and Research," the committee advises that adequate initial reading instruction requires a focus on:

- using reading to obtain meaning from print;
- the sublexical (phonological and morphological) components of words;
- the nature of the orthographic system;
- the specifics of frequent, regular spelling–sound relationships;
- frequent opportunities to read; and
- opportunities to write.

Furthermore, the committee advises that adequate progress in learning to read English beyond the initial level depends on:

- sufficient practice in reading to achieve fluency with different kinds of texts written for different purposes; and
- control over procedures for monitoring comprehension and repairing misunderstandings (Snow, Burns, & Griffin, 1998, p. 314).

We suggest that the last bulleted item, "Control over procedures for monitoring comprehension and repairing misunderstandings," assumes that students know how to use information from the semantic and syntactic cueing systems. The rest of the bulleted entries, however, focus on the graphophonemic system. As you plan instruction for your primary age students, we urge you to consider the number of elements in the Committee's list that focus on the acquisition of graphophonemic knowledge. It is the balance of these elements of instruction with those discussed in many other chapters of this book that are important to the goal that all of your students become readers who can read the words accurately and quickly and, at the same time, understand and find what they are reading meaningful.

Summary

Competency 6.1 advises that teachers help their students learn to use syntactic, semantic, and graphophonemic relations to monitor their identification of words. Our discussion includes an explanation of the triple cueing system, as well as the cautions of several researchers who have concerns about the importance of the graphophonemic system. Advice for how to balance the instructional implications of this often conflicting information is provided in the "What Does This Mean for You, the Teacher" section.

REFERENCES

*Recommended for teachers

*Adams, M. J. (1990). *Beginning to read: Thinking and learning about print—a summary*. Urbana, IL: University of Illinois at Urbana-Champaign, Center for the Study of Reading.

*Adams, M. J. (1998). The three-cueing system. In J. Osborn & F. Lehr (Eds.), *Literacy for all: Issues in teaching and learning*. New York: Guilford.

Clay, M. M. (1988). *The early detection of reading difficulties*. Auckland, New Zealand: Heinemann Educational Books.

Durkin, D. (1998). *Teaching them to read*. Boston, MA: Allyn & Bacon.

*Goodman, K. S. (1986). *What's whole in whole language?* Portsmouth, NH: Heinemann.

Graves, M. F., Juel, C., & Graves, B. B. (1998*). Teaching reading in the 21st century*. Boston, MA: Allyn & Bacon.

Heilman, A. W., Rupley, W., & Blair, T. (1998). *Principles and practices of teaching reading*. Englewood Cliffs, NJ: Prentice-Hall.

National Reading Panel. (2000). *Teaching children to read: An evidence-based assessment of the scientific research literature on reading and its implications for reading instruction*. Washington, DC: National Institute of Child Health and Human Development.

Routman, R. (1994). *Invitations: Changes as teachers and learners K–12*. Portsmouth, NH: Heinemann.

*Snow, C. E., Burns, M. S., & Griffin, P. (Eds.). (1998). *Preventing reading difficulties in young children*. Washington, DC: National Academy Press.

7 Phonics

COMPETENCY 6.2
Use phonics to teach students to use their knowledge of letter/sound correspondence to identify sounds in the construction of meaning.

Interpretation

We find the wording of this competency to be confusing. We do not think that, as written, it really states the intended competency. Our interpretation of the competency is as follows: Teach students to use phonics, which is knowledge of letter and sound correspondences, to identify words so as to construct meaning.

Related Research

Definition and Purpose of Phonics Instruction

The authors of the influential report, *Becoming a Nation of Readers*, offered a straightforward definition of phonics: "Phonics is instruction in the relationship between letters and speech sounds." Accompanying this definition is some good advice: "The goal of phonics instruction is not that children be able to state the 'rules' governing letter–sound relationships. Rather, the purpose is to get across the alphabetic principle, the principle that there *are* systematic relationships between letters and sounds." The report also advises that phonics "ought to be conceived as a technique for getting children off to a fast start in mapping the relationships between letters and sounds" (Anderson, Hiebert, Scott, & Wilkinson, 1985, p. 38). And it cautions that, once the basic relationships have been taught, the best way to get children to refine and extend their knowledge of letter–sound correspondences is through repeated opportunities to read.

A report from the National Research Council, *Preventing Reading Difficulties in Young Children*, recommends that first-grade instruction be designed to provide (among other things) "familiarity with spelling sound correspondences and common spelling conventions, and their use in identifying printed words" (Snow, Burns, & Griffin, 1998, p. 194). Furthermore, the report proposes that all first-grade children should be able to "accurately decode orthographically regular, one-syllable words and nonsense words using print–sound mappings to sound out unknown words," and "use letter–sound correspondence knowledge to sound out unknown words when reading text" (Snow, Burns, & Griffin, 1998, p. 81).

Preventing Reading Difficulties defines decoding as the aspect of the reading process that involves deriving a pronunciation for a printed sequence of letters. Essential to this aspect is knowledge of spelling–sound correspondences. Children who learn to "break the code" are able to read most of the words in their spoken language, and to independently figure out the pronunciations of many unknown words as well.

Research on the Effectiveness of Phonics Instruction

Preventing Reading Difficulties in Young Children addresses the controversial issue of the role of phonics in beginning reading instruction by summarizing a number of reviews of the research on this topic that have been carried out during the past forty years. Some of them are briefly discussed below.

1. *The Cooperative Research Program in First Grade Reading Instruction* compared different approaches to beginning reading instruction. This 1967 large-scale evaluation found a consistent advantage for code-emphasis approaches, while conceding that a single method is not necessarily the best for all children. But the researchers found that classroom programs that emphasized systematic phonics instruction and meaningful reading and writing surpassed those classrooms that centered on mainstream basal programs (Bond & Dykstra, 1967).

2. *Learning to Read: The Great Debate.* Chall's 1967 book included a review and analysis of the available research on instructional practices associated with beginning reading and found strong advantages for programs that included systematic phonics, especially for children from lower socioeconomic backgrounds. She emphasized the need for children to practice reading, with material both at the child's reading level as well as challenging material, so as to develop fluency.

3. *Beginning to Read: Thinking and Learning about Print.* In her 1990 book, Marilyn Adams assembles and analyzes studies about beginning reading that had been conducted both before and after the Chall report, as well as investigations of the psychological and language-based processes of reading. Adams concluded that direct instruction in phonics, focusing on the regularities of English orthography, was important to effective reading instruction, and that other factors, such as lots of practice reading and considerable attention to the acquisition of vocabulary, were also important.

Despite the twenty-three years that separate the Chall and Adams reports, their findings are highly convergent. The additional investigations that were conducted between 1967 and 1990 have only confirmed the importance of teaching children about how letters work in written words. It should also be noted, however, that neither Chall nor Adams advocates phonics instruction as the sole component of a program of beginning reading instruction. They both point to the importance of wide reading to reading proficiency.

The members of the National Reading Panel (2000) examined seventy-five studies involving phonics instruction and derived their conclusion about the effectiveness of phonics instruction from the thirty-eight studies that met their standards of scientific rigor. Their findings "provide strong evidence substantiating the impact of systematic phonics instruction on learning to read" (p. 2-92).

Of central importance is the finding that systematic phonics instruction contributed more than nonsystematic phonics instruction in helping kindergarten and first-grade children spell words. Furthermore, the Panel found that systematic phonics instruction is beneficial to students across social classes. In response to an often-voiced concern about phonics instruction—that it interferes with children's ability to read and understand—the Panel found that "Growth in reading comprehension is boosted by systematic phonics instruction for younger students and reading disabled students" (p. 2-94).

Of particular interest to primary grade teachers is the finding that phonics instruction that begins in kindergarten and first grade is more effective than phonics instruction introduced after first grade. Also of interest is that phonics instruction is equally effective in tutoring, small group, or whole class situations.

We will add another report to this array of reports: *Becoming a Nation of Readers* (Anderson, et al., 1985). This widely circulated report advocates an interactive view of reading by defining it as "a process in which information from the text and the knowledge possessed by the reader act together to produce meaning" (Anderson et al., 1985, p. 8). The report identifies five generalizations, based on the research of the previous decade, that describe the nature of reading. A brief synopsis of the first two of these generalizations follows.

1. Reading is a constructive process. To gain meaning, readers must combine their own knowledge with the topic of the text.
2. Reading must be fluent. Decoding skill must develop to the point where it is automatic and requires little conscious attention. Readers must be able to decode words quickly and accurately so that this process can be coordinated with the process of constructing meaning.

The second generalization is particularly notable as support for Competency 6.2. This generalization emphasizes the importance of quick and accurate decoding skill to the development of comprehension.

What Does This Mean for You, the Teacher?

Children who learn to use information about the relationships between letters and sounds to identify known words become independent readers who can, on their own, figure out unfamiliar words. Several aspects of phonics instruction are of particular importance in providing the kind of instruction that will enable children to become independent readers, and should be considered as you plan phonics instruction for your students.

1. Assess Your Students' Knowledge of Letters and Sounds. Instruction that focuses on letter and sound relationships assumes that children have some knowledge of the alphabet and of the sounds of spoken words. As numerous researchers have established and many teachers have observed, kindergarten and first-grade children enter school with different amounts and levels of knowledge about letters and sounds. (Many of these studies are reported in Snow, et al., 1998 and Adams, 1990.) Decades of studies have confirmed that children's well-developed letter knowledge (which includes identifying and writing letters), as well as their phonemic awareness (which includes their ability to hear and manipulate the separable sounds in spoken words) predict ease in learning to read.

Children who do not identify letters quickly and cannot write them easily need help in acquiring these skills. You can help your students learn the names of the letters by teaching them the well-known alphabet song and then helping them learn to attach the letter names they are learning to specific letter shapes (Adams, 1990, p. 65). In addition, you can offer lots of gamelike practice that centers on identifying and writing letters. Still somewhat controversial is how you can most effectively help your students develop phonological and phonemic awareness. (Further discussion of phonemic awareness appears in Chapter 24.)

2. Promote the Understanding of the Alphabetic Principle. Children's knowledge of letter–sound relationships is important to their learning to read English because of the alphabetic nature of written English. Written English has consistent, if not always perfectly predictable, relationships between letters and sounds. For example, the letter "m" almost always represents the sound /m/. A number of spelling patterns are also quite consistent. For example, the spelling "ea" stands for the "long e" sound in a lot of words: *bead, beam, bean, mean, scream, stream, team,* and many more.

You can promote an understanding of the alphabetic principle in many ways. For example, you can help your students focus on the relationships between single letters, or letter clusters, and the sounds they represent. You can emphasize frequently occurring spelling patterns, so as to show your students how these patterns affect the pronunciation of words. You can work with onsets and rimes.

3. Provide Word Recognition and Decoding Instruction. As your students learn the relationships between letters and sounds they must also learn how these relationships work to permit them to recognize words. Your decoding instruction can help your students understand how letter–sound relationships operate in combination, and how to apply their letter–sound and spelling pattern knowledge to read words.

How does decoding instruction look? You can use a variety of instructional activities that will provide students with information they can use as they read. For example, regularly play "word change" games by changing the beginning, middle, or ending letters in lists of regularly spelled words and having your students read the new words as the letters change.

- Help your students learn to use their letter–sound knowledge to "say the sound" of each letter in regularly spelled words and then combine, or blend, those sounds together to produce the pronunciations of the words.

Here is how a first-grade child puts this instruction to use: She is reading a story about a boy with muddy feet. She stops when she sees the word mat. *She knows the sounds of the consonants /m/ and /t/, and the "short" sound of the vowel /a/. She knows she can "say the sounds" of those letters, and that by combining those sounds, she will be able to pronounce the word. She reads* mat.

- Show your students how to combine onsets (the initial consonant or consonant cluster in a one-syllable word) and rimes (the vowel and the remainder of the word).

Here is how a first-grade boy who is reading a story about a child who plants a garden used what he knows about onsets and rimes. The boy stops when he sees the word bean. *He remembers "word work" they did in class with their teacher. She had shown them a list of words that looked very similar. They learned to separate the first part of a word and to look at the spelling of the second part. They practiced with several words:* mean, lean, Jean, Dean, *so now he separates the first letter from the word, "b" (the onset), and then looks at and remembers the pronunciation of the spelling pattern "ean" (the rime). He reads the word* bean.

- Help your students learn to identify frequently used spelling patterns that appear in longer words.

Here is how a first-grade girl goes about reading a two-syllable word. She stops when she sees the word blinking. *She looks at the end of the word because she knows that* -ing *is a separate part of the word, and that it frequently comes at the end of a word. She concentrates on the first part of the word. She knows that /b/ and /l/ combine to make the first sound of the word, and remembers that "ink" is a spelling pattern they have worked on in her reading group. She reads "blink . . . ing, blinking."*

4. Provide Lots of Practice. So that your students can focus on the meaning of what they are reading, they must be able to recognize most of the words they encounter quickly, accurately, and automatically. You can help your students gain both speed and accuracy by giving them lots of practice reading stories and other texts that contain lots of words they know how to decode, and other words they have learned as irregular words. You will find that their skill at decoding will permit them to get approximate pronunciations of words they have not previously seen in print.

5. Reflect on Some Unresolved Issues:

How much phonics? Because the importance of understanding the alphabetic principle is so fundamental to reading an alphabetic language, a number of program developers have worked on programs designed to teach phonics. These programs can differ from one another in significant ways. Some advocates of phonics instruction propose elaborate schemes for the teaching of hundreds of letter–sound relationships. Their claim is that children should learn all of these relationships before beginning to read words and stories.

A more research-based view of phonics instruction is contained in the advice given in *Becoming a Nation of Readers:* Phonics instruction should include only the most important and regular of letter-to-sound relationships. Importantly, and consistent with the recommendations of the other reports, the Commission further advised that, once the basic relationships have been taught, "the best way to get children to refine and extend their knowledge of letter–sound correspondences is through repeated opportunities to read" (Anderson et al., 1985, p. 38).

Phonics instruction is the topic of a number of books written especially for teachers (for example, Cunningham, 2000, Heilman, 1998, and Powell & Hornsby, 1993). These books attempt to provide coherent approaches to phonics instruction. They vary in approach and explicitness, but are often useful additions to discussions of phonics instruction in reading methods textbooks, or even the phonics instruction presented in basal reading programs.

How fast? How many? In what order? There are no "rules" that tell us how quickly or how slowly to introduce letter–sound relationships, in what order to introduce them, or how many should be taught. But, again, the contemporary view is that sound–letter relationships should be selected so that children can read words as soon as possible. This means that a carefully selected set of letters should be introduced and then combined into words that the children read, thus demonstrating to them the usefulness of learning letter–sound relationships. Therefore, it is important to avoid programs of instruction that feature large numbers of letter–sound relationships that are to be learned before the children read words, sentences, and stories. Also avoid programs (and informal practices) that present all of the consonants before any of the vowels, or, conversely, all of the vowels before any of the consonants. Both consonants and vowels are needed to form words.

Explicit or implicit? Approaches to letter–sound instruction differ in their focus. One approach is called "implicit" or "analytic," because the children learn to identify the sounds of individual letters or clusters of letters in the context of whole words. Another approach is called "explicit" or "synthetic" because the children first learn to identify the sounds of individually presented letters and then blend them together to make whole words.

A teacher using the analytic approach might begin her lesson by saying,

Let's read these words and then write she, shoe, ship, shelf *on the chalkboard. She and the children read the words, and then she asks, "Who can tell me the letters that make the sound you hear at the beginning of each of those words?" The children respond, and then she says, "the letters 'sh' make the sound that we hear at the beginning of* she, ship, shelf, *and* shoe. *Let's read those words again."*

In contrast, a teacher using an explicit approach to phonics instruction might start her lesson by writing three letters on the board, "m," "t," and "a."

She says, pointing to 'm,' *"We're going to learn the sound of this letter today. Tell me the name of this letter." The children identify the letter. Then the teacher says, "Listen to the sound this letter makes: mmmmmmmm. Let's all say it." The children respond, "mmmmm." The teacher points to the other two letters saying "You have learned the sounds of these letters. Let's go over them." She points to the "t," the children say /t/. Then she points to the "a" and says, "Tell me the sound we learned for this letter." The children respond with the sound of short /a/, the sound they learned earlier in the week.*

Which approach is the most useful? Each approach has advantages and disadvantages. The implicit approach helps children keep in mind that sounds and letters exist in words, but some children have trouble getting the point of the instruction because they have trouble separating out the sounds represented by the letters in the written words they are shown. For such children, this instruction becomes problematic, particularly when they are asked to identify sounds in the middle of words.

On the other hand, the disadvantage of the explicit approach is that many sounds cannot be said without adding a vowel sound, for example /d/ becomes *duh.* A second problem involves blending. It is important that programs of explicit phonics instruction include blending activities so that the children learn how to blend together the sounds they derive from the print they are reading. For example, a first-grade child who can successfully say the sound of each letter in the word *mat*, also has to know how to blend those stretched out sounds together to form the word *mat*.

Becoming a Nation of Readers reviewed both approaches and recommended that the most useful strategies were to isolate the sounds associated with most letters and to teach children to blend the sounds of letters together to try to identify words. These are the strategies of explicit phonics. But in indicating that there was insufficient justification for strictly adhering to one approach, the report suggests that teachers draw from both as needed (Anderson et al., 1985).

What about irregular, high-frequency words? Most programs of reading instruction include the gradual introduction of a number of "irregular" words that are taught as whole words or "sight" words. Words such as *have*, *said*, *was*, and *ought* are labeled "irregular" because they are difficult to read using a sounding out strategy. It is generally agreed that irregular words be introduced in a reasonable sequence and at a reasonable rate and that they should be continuously reviewed in the materials the children read.

Should phonics instruction be systematic (designed to provide children with an organized program of instruction) or incidental (based on the perceived needs of the children)? The answers to this important question vary. Some argue that the systematic instruction that can be found in an already published program of instruction is important for most children (if the program is good), whereas others argue that phonics instruction should be provided by teachers as they observe their students' efforts to read (if the teachers are sensitive to what children need to know about letters and sounds and if they are skilled at providing this kind of instruction). Many of the arguments about phonics instruction center on this question: should phonics instruction be systematic or incidental? We will avoid those arguments by saying that each of the reports we have discussed either directly recommends or implies a systematic program of phonics instruction, modified, of course, according to the needs of the children and the experiences of their teachers.

What kind of practice? Children need opportunities to practice accurate and fluent reading in stories and other texts. The phrase *decodable text* is used to describe stories and other materials that use the letter–sound relationships the children are learning as well as a limited number of high-frequency sight words. Decodable text may also contain a limited number of "story words" to make the text more interesting. Many children benefit from practice with stories and other texts that contain a high proportion of decodable and other familiar words.

Other kinds of texts found in beginning reading programs include predictable and patterned books. These books, written with repeated sentence patterns, provide print and language experiences that children enjoy, but typically they are not based on the sound–letter relationships, spelling patterns, and sight words that are being introduced in the program. For some children, the opportunities to apply what they are learning as they read in decodable books is critical. Alternatively, a number of programs offer "leveled" texts, books that have been graded according to difficulty by teachers and program developers.

Summary

In summary, we emphasize that the purpose of phonics instruction is to get across the alphabetic principle, the principle that there are systematic relationships between letters and sounds. Furthermore, with the authors of *Becoming a Nation of Readers*, we urge you to conceive of phonics instruction as a technique for getting children off to a fast start in mapping the relationships between letters and sounds.

Finally, we emphasize the recommendations about reading practice that were in each of the major reports cited in this chapter: Children engaged in phonics instruction must also be given large amounts of reading practice in books and other materials. And we urge that the chapters in Section 3, which focus on the comprehension competencies, be considered in their relationship to the competencies related to phonics instruction.

R E F E R E N C E S

*Recommended for teachers
*Adams, M. J. (1990). *Beginning to read: Thinking and learning about print.* Cambridge, MA: M.I.T. Press.
*Anderson, R., Heibert, E., Scott, J., & Wilkinson, I. (1985). *Becoming a nation of readers.* Urbana, IL: University of Illinois at Urbana-Champaign, Center for the Study of Reading.
Bond, G. L., & Dykstra, R. (1967). The cooperative research program in first grade reading instruction. *Reading Research Quarterly*, 2, pp. 5–142.
Chall, J. S. (1967). *Learning to read: The great debate.* New York: McGraw-Hill.
Cunningham, P. M. (2000). *Phonics they use: Words for reading and writing*, 3rd ed. New York: Longman.
Heilman, A. W. (1998). *Phonics in proper perspective*, 8th ed. Upper Saddle River, NJ: Merrill.
National Reading Panel. (2000). *Teaching children to read: An evidence-based assessment of the scientific research literature on reading and its implications for reading instruction.* Washington, DC: National Institute of Child Health and Human Development.
Powell, D., & Hornsby, D. (1993). *Learning phonics and spelling in whole language classrooms.* New York: Scholastic Professional Books.
Snow, K., Burns, M. S., & Griffin, P. (Eds.). (1998). *Preventing reading difficulties in young children.* Washington, DC: National Academy Press.

8 Context

COMPETENCY 6.3
Teach students to use context to identify and define unfamiliar words.

Interpretation

One dictionary defines context as, "the part or parts of a written or spoken passage preceding or following a particular word or group of words and so intimately associated with them as to throw light on their meaning" (*Webster's*, 1964, p. 492). Competency 6.3 implies two separate uses of the word *context*. The first is that students will use the context of a sentence or a passage to help them identify any words that are unfamiliar in print, that is, words that they cannot decode. The second is that they will use the context of the passage or sentence to define or figure out the meanings of words they can decode, but do not understand. Competency 6.3 also implies a third situation in which context is to be used, and that is when a student can neither pronounce a word nor understand its meaning.

Whereas the first use of *context* in Competency 6.3 focuses on the identification (or pronunciation) of words, the second use exemplifies the dictionary definition of *context* as an aid to the understanding of words, that is "to throw light on their meaning."

Related Research

Some research indicates that better readers recognize words without relying on information from context and that it is the poorer readers who rely more on contextual information to help them recognize words. (See Adams, 1990 for a review of this research.) What do skilled readers rely on to recognize words? To answer this question, we will describe some of the word-identification characteristics of skilled readers. Skilled readers have learned to decode words rapidly and automatically. Their firm and ready knowledge of the connections between letters and sounds permits them to, as they read, process essentially every letter or frequently used patterns of letters in every word (Snow, Burns, & Griffin, 1998; Adams, 1990). These skilled readers depend on their rapid and accurate decoding to both recognize words and process their meanings. These processes are so rapid and automatic that input from less reliable contextual information is not needed for word identification (Stanovich, 1993). But skilled readers do use context to confirm the meanings of words, to modify their understandings of the meanings, and sometimes they use context to attempt to figure out the meanings of the less familiar and unfamiliar words they are reading.

What does the word-recognition skill of good readers imply for the design of reading instruction for young readers? This is not an easy question to answer. All students should certainly learn to decode words quickly and automatically. But how instruction can most effectively foster rapid and automatic word recognition is a topic of some disagreement among reading educators. Some of these disagreements center on the use of context, particularly as a word-reading strategy. Many reading educators propose teaching children how to use context to help them identify words that are unfamiliar in print. Other reading educators suggest that this is not a good strategy. Their concern is that encouraging young students to rely on context to identify words interferes with their learning to use print (and, specifically, letter–sound and spelling–sound relationships) as the first, most useful, and most reliable avenue to word identification. They cite studies that reveal that younger and poorer readers tend to overrely on context, in part because their decoding skill is not sufficiently developed. (See the discussion of letter–sound correspondence instruction in Chapter 7.)

It is helpful to think about the situation in which younger and poorer readers find themselves when they encounter an unknown word that they are expected to read. If they cannot recognize the word by sight, nor sound it out, they have several options. They can guess; they can ask for help from their teacher, their friends, or, if they are reading at home, a parent; they can rely on the context of the passage. It seems evident that, while it can be useful for teachers to prompt "smart" guessing, guessing should not be taught as a primary word-identification strategy. The drawbacks to relying on other people are fairly obvious: Too much of this kind of help will get in the way of students becoming self-sufficient and independent readers. The drawbacks to relying on contextual information are less obvious, and have to do with both word meaning and word identification.

The major problem with using context to help determine the meanings of unknown words is that context is often unreliable, and, sometimes, unaccessible. It is important to realize that it is often the less frequent words (the words that the children have not encountered in previous readings) that contribute the most information to a passage. Adams presents the dilemma: "Children depend on the meaning of the passage (the context) to infer the meaning of its less familiar words, yet the meaning of the passage depends disproportionately upon the meanings of its less frequent words" (Adams, 1990, p. 89). Despite the dilemma, or perhaps because of it, Adams emphasizes the important role context plays in helping children determine the meanings of words and recommends that students receive explicit instruction in the strategic use of context to help them understand what they read.

But Adams cautions against encouraging students to rely on context as a strategy for the identification or recognition of words. She observes that, when the context is strong enough to permit students to quickly identify an unfamiliar word, they will have little incentive to study its spelling. She also points out that the use of context to help students correctly identify a word in one story may not prepare them to identify that same word when it appears in another story. In contrast, she cites the importance of teachers working with students to study the spellings of words the students do not recognize, so that they will increase their familiarity with these words.

Some more cautionary advice that relates to the use of context for word identification is offered in *Preventing Reading Difficulties in Young Children* (Snow, Burns, & Griffin, 1998). This report suggests that, when working with beginning readers, teachers should encourage students to sound out and confirm the identities of any visually unfamiliar words they encounter as they read. The authors' advice is that students should be "recognizing words primarily through attention to their letter–sound relationships." They further remark that: "Although context and pictures can be used as a tool to monitor word recognition, children should not be taught to use them to substitute for information provided by the letters in the word" (Snow, Burns, & Griffin, 1998, pp. 322–323).

Adams corroborates this general advice with some very specific advice. She suggests that teaching young children to use context to minimize letter–sound processing is not a very good strategy, but proposes that teachers can help students learn to combine contextual information with their developing knowledge of letter–sound correspondences. As children become more expert in applying their letter–sound knowledge, they will be able to sound out and then identify almost any written word that is in their listening vocabulary. Adams points out that the very process of sounding out a word necessarily involves the careful study of its spelling. By sounding out words students create a memory for their spellings that is supported by their knowledge of their pronunciation and meaning (Adams, 1990).

What Does This Mean for You, the Teacher?

The many uses of context that you are likely to employ to help your students read words and understand them have their origin in some long-standing instructional practices, many of which have been emphasized for years in reading methods textbooks and the teacher's guides in published programs of reading instruction. You will be offered many suggestions, many of which originate in common sense and good practice. Here are a few examples.

1. To help students who cannot pronounce or mispronounce a word in a story they are reading aloud, teachers can advise them to "use the meanings of the rest of the words in the sentence to help you say the word you don't know."
2. Some teachers utilize a variation of this advice, for example, "Look at the first letter of the word you don't know, read to the end of the sentence, and then use the sound of the first letter and the context to help you read that hard word."

3. Because illustrations are often considered to be a part of the context of a story, teachers are encouraged to urge their students to gather information from the picture. For example, "Look at the picture. It may help you with that hard word."
4. When their students read a word correctly but appear not to understand it, teachers make a general suggestion: "Read that sentence again. What do you think that word means? What makes sense?" Or they may ask questions about a story detail, "You read that word, *container*. Do you remember the girl's birthday present? It came wrapped in a very big box. A big box can be called a big container."

The first three examples illustrate how teachers use context to help students identify words. The fourth shows how teachers use context to help students understand the meaning of a word. You are likely to use both senses of the word *context* to help your students during reading instruction, but it is of primary importance that you become very conscious of what uses you are encouraging your students to make of context.

We believe that research indicates the importance of your encouraging students to become strategic and independent users of the context of the texts they are reading to determine the meanings of words and phrases. As your students read sentences and passages, you can help them learn to use the context of the texts they are reading to recall the meanings of words, to learn new meanings, and to appreciate the subtly varying uses of words. This kind of instruction will expand your students' understanding of the words and of the texts they are reading and will help them become independent readers.

We believe the same research indicates that you should be moderate in your promotion of context to help your students identify or recognize unfamiliar words. There will certainly be times when you will urge them to utilize this kind of information so as to quickly identify an unfamiliar word. But to routinely encourage your students to rely on the context of a sentence or a passage to identify the pronunciation of an unfamiliar word is probably a shortsighted instructional practice. Instead, you should help them become more expert users of the information in printed words. "Missed words" provide you with good opportunities to help your students refine and practice their decoding skill.

A number of reading educators have described different ideas for helping students learn how to use context to enrich their understanding of what they are reading. Many of these educators talk about "context clues." One suggestion is that students learn to differentiate the information that can be obtained between general context (the main topic of the passage) and local context (the words, phrases, and sentences in the passage). Other suggestions are that students learn to use typographical clues (parentheses, dashes, commas, quotation marks) to help them spot any definitions and synonyms in the text, pictorial and graphic information (maps, diagrams, charts, etc.) to help them understand the general context, syntactic clues (the use of grammar and usage) to determine the kinds of words that would be appropriate, and semantic clues (knowledge of word meanings) to make inferences about the meanings of words (Durkin, 1983).

As you work with your students, you will become more aware of the variety of methods you can use to develop your students' abilities to use context as a strategy for developing meaning. Because the opportunities to encourage students to use context most often occur as they are reading aloud, it is important to consider how you can most effectively carry out this kind of instruction. In helping one or more of your students to use context, you will have interrupted their reading so as to work on a word or a phrase. Whether this interruption is to help them identify a word or to determine the meaning of a word or phrase, it is still an interruption. You should be aware that such efforts, even when successful, are very likely to disrupt the flow of comprehension. For that reason, you should always encourage your students to reread sentences in which they "worked on words" so as to recover their comprehension.

What about having students skip words that are difficult for them to read? Given that a text is at an appropriate level of difficulty, it is preferable that students be encouraged not to skip difficult words. On the contrary, when students encounter a word that is hard to read, you should encourage them to take the time to study it. In addition to helping them examine its spelling, you can urge them to consider its meaning, using the information from both the context of the sentence and the passage.

A final note: Children do not benefit from reading texts that are excessively difficult. If children are having trouble with lots of words, you should provide them with easier texts.

Summary

Competency 6.3 focuses on the uses of context: Teachers are urged to teach their students to use context to both identify and define unfamiliar words. The research that supports the use of context as a strategy to figure out the meaning of unknown words is convincing. However, the use of context as a strategy to identify words has less research support, although it has an established basis in classroom practice. We suggest that an overreliance on context for the identification of words can distract young children from learning to use print as the most reliable means of identifying words.

R E F E R E N C E S

*Recommended for teachers
*Adams, M. J. (1990). *Beginning to read: Thinking and learning about print—a summary.* Urbana, IL: University of Illinois at Urbana-Champaign, Center for the Study of Reading.
Durkin, D. (1983). *Teaching them to read.* Boston, MA: Allyn & Bacon.
Snow, K., Burns, M. S., & Griffin, P. (Eds.). (1998). *Preventing reading difficulties in young children.* Washington, DC: National Academy Press.
*Stanovich, K. E. (1993). Romance and reality. *The Reading Teacher, 47*(4), 280–291.
Webster's Third New International Dictionary. (1961). Springfield, MA: G. & C. Merriam.

9 Connecting Reading, Writing, and Spelling

COMPETENCY 6.4
Guide students to refine their spelling knowledge through reading and writing.

COMPETENCY 6.5
Teach students to recognize and use various spelling patterns in the English language as an aid to word identification.

Interpretation

We discuss these two competencies together because of their reciprocal relationship. The first competency implies that teachers will use the instructional opportunities associated with reading and writing to help their students acquire knowledge of the spelling conventions of written language. The second competency implies that teachers will help their students utilize the frequently used spelling patterns of written English to help them identify words in print. In other words, Competency 6.4 supports the use of reading and writing to improve students' ability to spell words, whereas Competency 6.5 supports the use of spelling to improve students' ability to read words.

Related Research

The instructional relationships among spelling, writing, and reading are well established (see, for example, Snow, Burns, & Griffin, 1998; National Reading Panel, 2000). Almost all current approaches to reading instruction emphasize the importance of children learning to write and to spell as they are learning to read. (See, for example, Fountas & Pinnell, 1996; Au, Mason, & Scheu, 1995; Heilman, Blair, & Rupley, 1998.) Although the inclusion of writing and spelling as important components of reading instruction has been emphasized in recent years, the concept is not new. In fact, some educators have observed that many children begin learning to read by writing. Many years ago, Maria Montessori advocated that children should write before reading (Montessori, 1966), and in a classic study of children who learned to read before entering school, Durkin found that many of the children she studied learned to write before they learned to read. She commented that "the ability to read seemed almost like a by-product of the ability to print and spell" (Durkin, 1966, p. 137).

It is difficult to talk about children's writing without also talking about how they learn to spell words. Many children begin to spell words as they are learning about the relationships of letters to the sounds of spoken words and are attempting to use this knowledge in writing labels and messages. Young children may use drawings and single letters to convey their messages, but as they learn more about spelling and writing, they begin to include words with more letters in them. They often devise or invent spellings that may not be correct but that have a direct relationship to the sounds of the words they hear in the words they are attempting to write. For example, in a sentence about a mouse, a child may spell *mouse* with the letters "ms."

Invented Spellings

In recent years, a great deal of instructional interest has centered on the "invented spellings" of children who are learning to read and write. What is the relationship of children's phonemic awareness (that is, their awareness of the separate sounds of spoken words) to their knowledge of how words are spelled? Does phonemic awareness develop as children work to figure out spellings on their own? A great deal of research (for example, see Templeton & Morris, 1999) supports the value of children spending time discovering and/or "inventing" spellings of words they want to write. It is important to recognize, however, that this discovery process is subject to many influences. In describing how one young boy was learning to write an increasing number of words, one researcher noted several interrelated influences on this process: the boy's interest in conveying information in writing, his phonemic awareness, his increasing knowledge of "the tool of phonics," and the help of his mother (Hansen, 1998, p. 216).

Some common features of the invented spellings of children have been studied and identified. For example, because they are auditorially more apparent, consonants typically appear first and vowels appear later (Templeton & Morris, 1999). Some additional features of invented spellings include that children often use the names of the letters to represent a word or part of a word, for example *while* may be spelled "yl," and *can* may be spelled "kn." When children begin to write vowels, they typically let long vowels "speak for themselves," for example, *tail* may be spelled "tal," *use* may be spelled "us." Children often write short vowel letters that come close to the sound they hear, for example, they may spell *fall* as "foll." They may leave the vowel letter out, for example, *miss* may be spelled "mss." The letters "l" and "r" tend to lose their accompanying vowels, for example, *curl* is spelled "crl" and *butter* is spelled "butr" (Adams, 1990, p. 96).

The Spelling System of Written English

Templeton and his colleagues (Henderson & Templeton, 1986; Templeton & Morris, 1999) describe three layers of information in the spelling system of written English—the alphabetic layer, the pattern layer, and the meaning layer—and define them as follows:

> The alphabetic layer—In English, there are a good number of words whose spellings are primarily left to right and are represented by a fairly straightforward matching of letters and sounds, for example, *mat, fun, last*.

> The pattern layer—The spellings of another group of English words provide information about sounds that a group or pattern of letters represents within syllables, for example, *ought, home, nation*, and also across syllables.

> The meaning layer—The consistent spelling of meaning elements within some words, despite sound changes, provides information about the meanings of these words, for example, *critic/criticize, please/pleasure* (Templeton & Morris, 1999, p. 105).

Learning about the Layers of Information

The invented spellings of young students provide the groundwork for them to develop familiarity with the alphabetic layer of information. The pattern layer is conceptually more advanced than the alphabetic layer and the meaning layer is the most advanced. Templeton and Morris propose that students' understandings of these layers of information develop over time, depending on their experiences with reading and writing, as well as the opportunities they are given to examine and explore words outside of actual reading and writing.

In summarizing the conclusions of a number of studies of children's spellings, Adams (1990) points out that, as students are learning to read, their writing will reflect their increasing knowledge of the accurate spellings of words and an increasing awareness of the phonemes in spoken words. During this period, children's writing comes to reflect what Templeton and Morris (1999) describe as an "alphabetic expectation." That is, students learn that the sounds within words are matched one-to-one with letters that are read from left to right. The spellings of the words like *map, stop*, and *fan* nicely satisfy their alphabetic expectations.

As students learn to read and write more words, however, they find out that this alphabetic expectation does not account for all of the spellings of written English. When students read more complex words, they learn that some words contain groups or patterns of letters that work together to represent sounds, and that some letters do not stand for sounds. They also learn other aspects of spelling patterns: For example, in the case of a silent "e" at the end of a one-syllable word (indicating a long vowel in the middle of the word), they learn to skip to the end of the word, and then to look backward. According to Templeton and Morris, an indication that children have understood this spelling pattern in reading is the appearance of "silent" letters in the words they write.

When evaluating the effect of systematic phonics instruction on children's growth in spelling, the members of the National Reading Panel found that systematic phonics instruction helped kindergarten and first-grade children apply their knowledge of the alphabetic system to spell words, but that such instruction did not improve the spelling of older students (2000, p. 2-95). This finding further supports the need for instructional attention to the pattern layer as children progress as spellers *and* as readers.

How important to successful reading and spelling is the acquisition of spelling patterns? The answer to that question is, "very important." Adams says, "Just as in good reading, good spelling seems to depend upon sensitivity to patterns of letters, rather than (only) individual letter–sound correspondences" (Adams, 1990, p. 101). She argues that the reading behavior of both good and poor spellers reflects differences in their knowledge of spelling patterns. Whereas good spellers recognize and utilize spelling patterns during reading, poor spellers tend to rely on the initial letters of words. Poor readers often correct errors by substituting words that may make sense, but that do not contain the same sounds as the words in the text.

In advocating that an awareness of spelling patterns helps students in both reading and spelling, Templeton and Morris write: "When students encounter an unknown word in reading they can apply their knowledge of patterns to access the sound of the word. When students are writing and are unsure of a spelling, they can attend to the sounds they hear to generate spellings" (1999, p. 64). Furthermore, they argue that when students move from relying only on alphabetic correspondences to learning some spelling patterns, the possibilities for correctly spelling both known and unknown words increase significantly.

As students progress through the grades, their knowledge of spelling patterns contributes to their understanding of the spellings of syllable patterns and syllable combinations. As students learn more about compound words, base or root words, prefixes and suffixes, they are introduced to the idea that spelling can convey information about the meaning of words.

The value of instruction in the meaning parts of words that are morphemes, or meaning-based units—root or base words, prefixes, suffixes—is supported by both research and practice (Stahl, 1999; Nagy, 1988; Templeton & Morris, 1999). "Indeed, the common spelling of derivationally related words may be one of the most efficient and effective means of becoming aware of and organizing concepts that share a common underlying conceptual domain" (Templeton & Morris, 1999, p. 106).

For example, the spelling of one word can provide information about the meanings of several related words, for example, *please, pleasing, pleasant,* and *pleasure.* Although the pronunciation of *please* changes across these words, the meanings of each of these words is related to the meaning (and spelling) of *please.* Thus, the common spellings of elements of meaning-related words are useful to students as they read and write. Many English words can be grouped according to the spellings of similar meaning elements.

How attention to the three layers of spelling information—alphabetic, patterns, and meaning—can positively affect students' reading as well as their writing is nicely summarized by Templeton and Morris. In concluding that there is consensus in the research community about the importance of these relationships, they write:

The process of *writing* words and the process of *reading* words draw upon the same underlying base of word knowledge. The more students understand about the structure of words—their spelling or orthography—the more efficient and fluent their reading will be. Thus, orthographic knowledge is the engine that drives efficient reading as well as efficient writing (1999, p. 103).

Adams also strongly supports spelling instruction as an important component of a program of reading instruction. She says: "Learning about spelling reinforces children's knowledge about common letter sequences. It also reinforces their knowledge about spelling–sound relationships and may help children become aware of word parts. Because of this, spelling practice enhances reading proficiency" (Adams, 1990, p. 103).

What Does This Mean for You, the Teacher?

If you are a kindergarten or first-grade teacher, we urge that you support the attempts of your students as they use their invented spellings to write words and sentences. We also urge that you consider these spellings as current and reliable information about progress as the students gain understanding of the relationships of sounds to the letters that represent them. You will see your students move gradually from invented spelling to alphabetic spelling as you encourage them to become more conscious of the sounds of spoken words and the letters that represent them.

Some parents worry about the invented spellings in the papers their children bring home from school. You should advise them of the advantages of encouraging children to develop these spellings, but assure them that their children are also learning (and are very interested in learning) how to spell conventionally. In urging that the use of invented spelling is "not in conflict with teaching correct spelling," the Committee on "The Prevention of Reading Difficulties in Young Children" (Snow, Burns, & Griffin, 1998, p. 195) supports the use of beginning writing with invented spelling as useful in several ways. This practice helps develop children's understandings of the identities of phonemes (sounds), their understanding of how phonemes can be segmented (separated) in spoken words, and their knowledge of sound–spelling relationships.

How long should you encourage invented spelling? Templeton and Morris (1999) advise that spelling pattern instruction should begin when students have attained full phonemic awareness, which they define as the ability to attend consciously to both consonants and vowels within written words. For most children this occurs about the middle of first grade. It is important to recognize that, during this transition from invented to alphabetic spelling, spelling instruction is likely to be closely related to phonics and word-identification instruction.

Although invented spelling activities will develop your students' phonemic awareness and promote their understanding of how letters represent sounds, such activities must not replace practice in reading and instruction in word recognition. (Adams, 1990). In advice intended for primary-grade teachers, the "Preventing Reading Difficulties" committee urges that primary-grade teachers develop their students' correct spelling through "focused instruction and practice" and advises that primary-grade children be expected "to spell previously studied words and spelling patterns correctly in their final writing products" (Snow, Burns, & Griffin, 1998, p. 195).

Adams (1990) suggests that, as they read, all children be encouraged to examine the spelling patterns of some of the troublesome words they encounter. She also suggests that teachers help their students learn about the spellings of these words, rather than just "telling" them the word. She advises: "Spelling–sound translations serve to create, confirm, and secure children's visual knowledge of spelling patterns. . . . On the other hand, when students gloss over the complete spelling of a word as they read, they miss the opportunity to learn its spelling more thoroughly" (Adams, 1990, p. 101).

What is the best way to help your students learn about spelling patterns? While it is important to point out the spellings of some of the new and important words that your students encounter as they are reading (and may want to use as they write), it is also important to offer your students some systematic and explicit instruction that focuses on spelling patterns and word exploration (Adams, 1990; Templeton & Morris, 1999). Adams suggests that, when you give your students separate practice in spelling and writing words, they will be able to devote their full attention to the spellings of these words. And when your students copy some words, their memory for the spellings of those words will be strengthened (Adams, 1990, p. 102).

In pointing out that most students do not discover the different layers of spelling patterns on their own, Templeton and Morris suggest three principles to use when selecting and organizing words for instruction:

1. The words you select should be developmentally appropriate, but you should focus on words with which the students are having problems. For example, if the students are confusing the letters that represent short vowel sounds, you can develop activities that provide them with practice on these particular letter and sound relationships.

2. Organize words for study according to their spelling patterns or meaning connections. For example, younger students can learn about vowel patterns such as those in the words *eat, flea, team, seat, beat*, or the words *tie, pie, lie*. Older students can learn more about combining root words with prefixes and suffixes. They can also learn about the meaning connections among words that have similar spellings such as *master, masterful, masterly, masterpiece*.

3. Organize spelling instruction so that, for the most part, students study words they are able to recognize automatically during reading. This is especially important for students in grades 1 through 3. Although most of the spelling words that students in grade 4 and beyond study should be words they know how to read, some new words should be introduced. These words should relate in both meaning and spelling to known words. So, for example, students who correctly spell and understand the meaning of the word *art* can be helped to learn the meanings and the spellings of the words *artful* and *artless*. Remember that most of your students are not likely to become aware of the spelling and meaning features of related words unless you point them out.

Templeton and Morris (1999) address several questions that are frequently asked about spelling instruction, especially by new teachers.

1. How many words should students be learning to spell each week? For students in the alphabetic stage (typically in the latter half of first grade), fewer than ten words per week is appropriate. The words should be organized around common features or patterns. Some high-frequency words necessary for writing should also be included. Second and third graders working in the within-word pattern level should study ten to twelve words a week. Fourth-grade students working on word syllables and meanings typically study twenty words per week. Frequently misspelled words and particular words the students wish to spell should be added to these groups of words, but the emphasis should be on the patterns inherent in the selected words.

2. Where can I find appropriate words for word study? Examine published spelling programs to see the extent to which they present features and patterns in an appropriate manner. Also, examine other resources for teachers that present words organized according to pattern, for example, Bear, Invernizzi, and Templeton (1996) or Henry (1996).

3. How do I determine my students' spelling levels? You can determine your students' spelling levels by using one of a number of commercially developed spelling inventories.

4. What types of instructional activities work best? As already discussed, the experiences of your students in both reading and writing will benefit their learning of spelling. In addition, most of your students will benefit from explicit spelling instruction. The advice from Templeton and Morris is very specific: "Explicit instruction involves teacher-directed as well as student-directed examination of words" (1999, p. 108). You are urged to organize words in ways that will help students understand how particular spelling features and patterns operate. Some further advice is also very specific: "Teacher-directed does not mean teaching spelling rules—in fact, trying to teach spelling through rules is one of the least effective approaches one can take" (1999, pp. 108–109). Rather, you should help your students see how letter patterns work in the spellings of words, and, later, how meaning patterns can help them learn both the spellings and the meanings of many words.

Specific activities include word sorts (in which students sort words according to spelling or meaning patterns). By providing your students with opportunities to compare, contrast, and classify words, you give them the chance to consider words from a variety of perspectives. Teacher-developed word and spelling games can be supplemented with commercially developed board games and card games that focus on words and spelling patterns.

5. What type of spelling strategies should be taught? As is true with most instruction, your students most easily learn something new when it is related to what they already know. For example, if students know how to spell *picture*, but misspell *nature*, you can help them become aware of the similarities in the pronunciation and spelling of the last syllable of each word. By showing your students how to take advantage of what they know, you are modeling a way of thinking about written words.

In recommending a "tried and true" strategy for learning the spellings of new words, Templeton and Morris cite the frequently offered advice of Horn (1969), which is to have your students *look, say,* and *write.* To this advice they add *think* and the strategy becomes *look, say, think,* and *write.* The *think* step involves your students thinking about similar words they already know as they work on the spellings of new words.

Finally, when you have your students correct misspelled words, it is important to show them how much of a misspelled word they already know how to spell. Templeton and Morris offer some very wise advice: "By first reinforcing what is correct and then moving to what needs to be fixed up, we show students *how* to look at their misspellings. They need to realize that they have not missed the whole word, but rather just a part of it—in effect, they already know most of the word" (1999, pp. 109–110).

6. How can I assess how my students are progressing? You can assess spelling progress in a number of different ways. You can examine student writing, administer spelling inventories at various times during the school year, give the tests that appear in commercially developed spelling programs, and make up your own weekly pretests and posttests. All of these measures can contribute to your knowledge of how your students are progressing in spelling. A word of caution: Some of your students may be able to memorize the spellings of the words in weekly spelling tests, yet rather consistently misspell these same words in their written work. This probably means that they are not learning and internalizing the underlying pattern knowledge that they need to be good spellers.

In contrast, when you offer your students an instructional emphasis that focuses on the exploration of the patterns that can be detected in the sound, structure, and meaning features of words—as opposed to a single-minded focus on learning how to spell the 5,000 most frequently occurring words in writing—you will help your students become both better spellers and better readers.

Summary

Competencies 6.4 and 6.5 urge teachers to take advantage of the reciprocal relationships among reading, writing, and spelling to refine the spelling knowledge of their students and also to aid in the development of their ability to identify words. The research and practice of the past decades have emphasized the close relationships among these three aspects of literacy and the importance of exploiting these relationships during reading and spelling instruction. Attention to these relationships is important at every level of learning in elementary school. When teachers support kindergarten children's early attempts to write messages with pictures, letters, and words, they not only are helping their students understand that writing can convey meaning, they are also helping them learn about spelling words and reading them. When teachers help their primary-level students understand the alphabetic nature and special letter patterns of many of the words they are learning to spell, they are helping them identify these words when they encounter them in print. When teachers of upper-elementary grade students help them learn about compound words, base words, and prefixes and suffixes, their students learn that information from word parts can contribute, not only to their knowledge of how words are spelled, but also to what those words mean. Helping students learn to pay attention to the relationships among reading, spelling, and writing will contribute to their understanding of each of these aspects of literacy.

R E F E R E N C E S

*Recommendations for teachers

*Adams, M. J. (1990). *Beginning to read: Thinking and learning about print—a summary.* Urbana: IL: University of Illinois at Urbana Champaign, Center for the Study of Reading.

Au, K. A., Mason, J. M., & Scheu, J. A. (1995). *Literacy instruction for today.* New York: Harper Collins.

Bear, D. R., Invernizzi, M., & Templeton, S. (1996). *Words their way: Word study for phonics, vocabulary, and spelling instruction.* Englewood Cliffs, NJ: Prentice-Hall.

Durkin, D. (1966). *Children who read early: Two longitudinal studies.* New York: Teachers College Press.

Fountas, J. C., & Pinnell, G. S. (1996). *Guided reading: Good first grade teaching for all children.* Portsmouth, NH: Heinemann.

Hansen, J. (1998). Young writers: the people and purposes that influence their literacy. In J. Osborn & F. Lehr (Eds.), *Literacy for all: Issues in teaching and learning* (pp. 205–236). New York: Guilford.

Heilman, A. W., Blair, T. R., & Rupley, W. H. (1998). *Principles and practices of teaching reading.* Upper Saddle River, NJ: Merrill.

Henderson, E. H., & Templeton, S. L. (1986). A developmental perspective of formal spelling instruction through alphabet, pattern, and meaning. *Elementary School Journal, 86,* 305–316.

Henry, M. K.(1996). *Words: Integrated decoding and spelling instruction based on word origin and structure.* Austin, TX: Pro-Ed.

Horn, T. (1969). Spelling. In R. L. Ebel (Ed.), *Encyclopedia of educational research* (4th ed., pp. 1282–1299). New York: Macmillan.

Montessori, M. (1966). *The secret of childhood.* New York: Ballantine.

Nagy, W. (1988). *Teaching vocabulary to improve reading comprehension.* Newark, DE, International Reading Association.

National Reading Panel. (2000). *Teaching children to read: An evidence-based assessment of the scientific research literature on reading and its implications for reading instruction.* Washington, DC: Department of Health and Human Services.

*Snow, K., Burns, M. S., & Griffin, P. (Eds.). (1998). *Preventing reading difficulties in young children.* Washington, DC: National Academy Press.

*Stahl, S. A. (1999). *Vocabulary development.* Cambridge, MA: Brookline Books.

*Templeton, S., & Morris, D. (1999). Questions teachers ask about spelling. *Reading Research Quarterly, 34*(1), 102–112.

10 Vocabulary

COMPETENCY 6.6
Employ effective techniques and strategies for the ongoing development of independent vocabulary acquisition.

Interpretation

This competency implies that teachers should use effective instructional techniques and strategies for the sole goal of helping children learn how to learn words—that is, learn how to acquire vocabulary in texts they read independently. However, most of the existing research on vocabulary focuses on how students "naturally" acquire word knowledge and how instruction can facilitate learning particular vocabulary from particular texts. Therefore, we think the intent of the competency is that teachers should use effective instructional techniques and strategies to help children learn new words and acquire greater knowledge of partially known words from classroom materials. Some, but not all, of these techniques and strategies may help children learn new vocabulary through independent reading.

Related Research

Research has established the following:

1. Knowledge of the meaning of words is strongly related to reading comprehension. Research has shown that this relationship is causal: Effective teaching of vocabulary will improve reading comprehension (Stahl & Fairbanks, 1986; National Reading Panel, 2000).

2. Children learn a great number of words in a year. Estimates vary, but most recent estimates suggest that children acquire 3,000 to 4,000 new words per year (Nagy & Anderson, 1984; Nagy & Herman, 1987; Stahl, 1999). Because probably only

about 300 to 500 words can be directly taught during a year (Stahl, 1999), instruction obviously does not account for all vocabulary learning. Children must acquire most vocabulary indirectly, through repeated exposures to words in various oral and written contexts.

3. People have varying levels of word knowledge. Because vocabulary knowledge grows gradually over time through repeated exposures, it follows that, at any point in time, people have varying levels of vocabulary knowledge. Four levels of word knowledge have been proposed by Dale and O'Rourke (1986): (1) I never saw it before; (2) I've heard of it, but I don't know what it means; (3) I recognize it in context; it has something to do with; (4) I know it. "Knowing" a word involves understanding its core meaning and how it changes in different contexts.

4. Context varies in helpfulness in establishing word meaning. Although children learn most vocabulary through repeated exposures to the words in context, explicit context cues are seldom available in oral language or written text. Beck, McKeown, and McCaslin (1983) suggest four levels of context helpfulness: (1) *Directive* contexts provide explicit and detailed information about the word; (2) *generally directive* contexts provide general information about the word; (3) *nondirective* contexts provide little or no information about the word; and (4) *misdirective* contexts promote misunderstandings about the word. Because of the limited usefulness of *single* contexts in providing information about word meaning, research on techniques of teaching people to learn from context (for example, using general guidance, specific strategies, cues, or lists of context cues) has generally been unsuccessful. Stahl (1999) concludes that, because learning from context is a process that children seem to do automatically, teaching strategies for learning from context may be unnecessary.

5. Understanding a word involves both definitional and contextual knowledge (Stahl, 1999). *Definitional knowledge* is knowledge of the logical relationship of the word to other words, such as the category or class to which it belongs, and its synonyms and antonyms. *Contextual knowledge* is knowledge of how the word's meaning changes with different contexts. For example, consider how the meaning of the *bear* homonyms changes with context in the following two sentences: "The mother bear cuffed her cub on the snout" and "I can't bear to see you suffering like this." As a subtler example, note how the meaning of the verb *give* changes in the following sentences: "The boxer gave his opponent a blow to his left temple" and "The mother gave her son a huge hug."

6. Learning occurs when students are actively involved in trying to connect new information to what they already know. Teaching to encourage such processing includes having students define new vocabulary in their own words, provide examples and nonexamples, and generate synonyms and antonyms.

The members of the National Reading Panel examined a number of vocabulary studies and found that a "variety of direct and indirect methods of instructional methods can be effective," and they offer the following implications for practice (2000, p. 4-27):

1. Vocabulary should be taught both directly and indirectly.
2. Repetition and multiple exposures to vocabulary items are important.
3. Learning in rich contexts is valuable for vocabulary learning.
4. Vocabulary tasks should be restructured when necessary.
5. Vocabulary learning should entail active engagement in learning tasks.
6. Computer technology can be used to help teach vocabulary.
7. Vocabulary can be acquired through incidental learning.
8. How vocabulary is assessed and evaluated can have differential effects on instruction.
9. Dependence on a single vocabulary instruction method will not result in optimal learning.

What Does This Mean for You, the Teacher?

The research described above, as well as additional studies on particular methods of vocabulary instruction, offer suggestions to you about how to teach vocabulary in your classroom. The most important message is that your students should read a great deal of text that provides challenging vocabulary. Here are some ways to accomplish that goal: (1) Establish a classroom library that allows your students easy access to many books at their reading level; (2) plan for students to visit the school library frequently; (3) set aside a daily period for independent reading (some elementary schools allocate thirty minutes or more per day for independent reading); (4) encourage parents to have their children read at home. The more children read, the more new and partially known words they will encounter, and the more word knowledge they will acquire (Cunningham & Stanovich, 1998).

You should also provide ample opportunities for children to hear complex and varied oral language in school. Plan to read aloud to your students every day from a variety of narrative and informational texts. Engage your students in conversations and discussions about these books.

Research has also suggested what you should teach and how you should teach it.

What to Teach

Because instructional time for vocabulary is a precious commodity, you cannot possibly provide intensive instruction for all new or incompletely known words. What words, then, should you focus on? Research provides three suggestions.

1. Teach conceptually difficult words. In school, students often encounter difficult concepts in particular disciplines when they read content area textbooks and other informational materials. Key concepts such as *democracy* and *ecosystem* are not only inherently difficult, but also they are often introduced with many other new, challenging terms. You should focus on teaching these conceptually difficult content vocabulary and related terms. You can leave other vocabulary for your students to

learn on their own as they read. You will thus be giving them needed practice with learning vocabulary independently.

2. Teach vocabulary that is important to the meaning of the text. For both informational and narrative text, some vocabulary is more important for comprehension than other vocabulary. Your instruction should focus on vocabulary that is important to understanding the text, rather than simply interesting novel vocabulary that is not closely related to the main idea of the selection. For example, in teaching the Greek myth of Narcissus, it is more important to devote instructional time to words such as *conceited* and *reflection* than *spellbound* or *yearn*. Your students may be able to infer the meanings of the latter two words.

3. Teach word parts. In addition to suggesting the type of words to teach, research also suggests that you should teach word parts—prefixes, suffixes, and root words. Instruction in word parts is especially useful for vocabulary related to content-area learning because much of this vocabulary repeatedly uses certain key root words.

Three reasons for teaching prefixes include the following (Graves & Hammond, 1980): (1) Relatively few prefixes are used in large numbers of words; about twenty prefixes account for nearly all prefixed words in school texts (White, Sowell, & Yanagihara, 1989); (2) most prefixes have easily definable and fairly constant meanings; (3) prefixes usually have consistent spellings. For these reasons, teaching a relatively small number of prefixes could result in significantly increased vocabulary learning.

As with prefixes, a relatively few suffixes account for most common meanings (White, Sowell, & Yanagihara, 1989). The most common suffixes are inflectional endings (*-s, -es*), verb endings (*-ed, -ing, -en*), and adjective endings (*-er, -est*). Other suffixes, such as *-ly, -ful, -ment*, and *-ness* are less common, but may still be useful to teach.

Research showing the advantage of teaching root words is sparse, and reading educators do not agree on whether root words should be taught at all, or, if so, when. However, if you help your students learn Greek and Latin root words, they may have an easier time learning and remembering related words. For particular content areas, teaching your students root words may be especially worthwhile (e.g., teaching the Greek root *geo* in an earth science class).

You should begin instruction in word parts with the idea that many words can be divided into parts that function together to give the word meaning. Then, your instruction should include the aspects of effective vocabulary instruction described in the next section.

How to Teach

The research on vocabulary instruction suggests that you should provide direct instruction in vocabulary in your reading program. To make vocabulary instruction effective, you should include three components: (1) provide definitional and contextual information; (2) actively involve children in word learning; and (3) provide multiple exposures to meaningful information about the word (Stahl, 1999).

Provide Definitional and Contextual Information.   Because understanding a word involves both definitional and contextual knowledge, your instruction should include both definitional and contextual information about word meaning. Teaching definitions alone is not a very effective way to promote reading comprehension (Stahl & Fairbanks, 1986), partly because dictionary definitions (1) often do not effectively convey new concepts, and (2) tell little about how a word is actually used in varying contexts (Nagy, 1988). However, you can provide definitional information by teaching synonyms and antonyms, providing examples and nonexamples, discussing differences between the target word and related words, and having students restate definitions in their own words. You can provide contextual information by discussing the meaning of the same word in different contexts and having students write their own contexts for the target word.

Research on direct instruction in deriving word meaning from context (e.g., teaching context clues, specific strategies, or general guidelines), however, has equivocal results. Several research reviews have concluded that instruction in learning vocabulary from context does not improve skill in word learning (Beck & McKeown, 1991; Graves, 1986; Kuhn & Stahl, 1998; Stahl, 1999). However, a recent meta-analysis of instructional studies on deriving word meaning from context (Fukkink & de Glopper, 1998) suggests that clue instruction (e.g., synonym, contrast, and illustration clues) may be more effective than other types of instruction or just practice. The authors caution, however, that research on instruction about deriving word meaning from context is still in its infancy and that we do not yet know specifically which clues are most effective and how many clues you should teach.

Actively Involve Children in Word Learning.   You should provide instruction that actively involves students and helps them relate the meaning of a new word to familiar concepts and experiences. For example, research suggests that you conduct open discussions of vocabulary, drawing on the expertise of various children. When you discuss complex concepts, you should actively involve students in grappling with word meaning. For example, you could use such approaches as semantic grouping, semantic mapping, semantic feature analysis, and comparing and contrasting.

Provide Multiple Exposures to Meaningful Information about the Word.   The richer and more extensive the instruction you provide in new words, the more your students' comprehension is likely to improve (McKeown, et al., 1985; Stahl & Fairbanks, 1986; National Reading Panel, 2000). In short, more is better, especially if your goal is to have students know a word to the extent that they can use it effectively in various contexts. In addition to teaching techniques already mentioned, McKeown and associates (1985) discuss other techniques that you can use to provide meaningful applications of new vocabulary. An example is questions that invoke possible relationships between two new vocabulary words, such as "Could a *miser* be *magnanimous?*" Another example is asking students to search for examples of target vocabulary in sources outside the classroom.

Summary

In summary, research related to vocabulary has established the strong relationship between word knowledge and reading comprehension, and has also suggested how people learn new words and hone their understanding of partially known words. The instructional implications of this research suggest *what* and *how* you can teach your students about unfamiliar words.

R E F E R E N C E S

*Recommended for teachers

Beck, I. L., & McKeown, M. G. (1991). Conditions of vocabulary acquisition. In R. Barr, M. L. Kamil, P. B. Mosenthal, & P. D. Pearson (Eds.), *Handbook of Reading Research*, vol. II (pp. 789–814). New York: Longman.

Beck, I. L., McKeown, M. G., & McCaslin, E. S. (1983). All contexts are not created equal. *Elementary School Journal, 83*, 177–181.

*Blachowicz, C., & Fisher, P. (1996). *Teaching vocabulary in all classrooms*. Upper Saddle River, NJ: Merrill.

Cunningham, A. E., & Stanovich, K. E. (1998). What reading does for the mind. *American Educator, 22*(1&2), 8–15.

Dale, E., & O'Rourke, J. (1986). *Vocabulary building*. Columbus, OH: Zaner-Bloser.

Fukkink, R. G., & de Glopper, K. (1998). Effects of instruction in deriving word meaning from context: A meta-analysis. *Review of Educational Research, 68*(4), 450–469.

Graves, M. F. (1986). Vocabulary learning and instruction. In E. Z. Rothkopf & L. C. Ehri (Eds.), *Review of Research in Education*, vol. 1 (pp. 49–89). Washington, DC: American Educational Research Association.

Graves, M., & Hammond, H. K. (1980). A validated procedure for teaching prefixes and its effect on students' ability to assign meanings to novel words. In M. Kamil & A. Moe (Eds.), *Perspectives on reading research and instruction* (pp. 184–188). Washington, DC: National Reading Conference.

Kuhn, M. R., & Stahl, S. A. (1998). Teaching children to learn word meanings from context: A synthesis and some questions. *Journal of Literacy Research, 30*(1), 1998, 119–138.

McKeown, M., Beck, I., Omanson, R., & Pople, M. (1985). Some effects of the nature and frequency of vocabulary instruction on the knowledge and use of words. *Reading Research Quarterly, 20*, 222–235.

*Nagy, W. E. (1988). *Teaching vocabulary to improve reading comprehension*. Newark, DE: International Reading Association.

Nagy, W. E., & Anderson, R. C. (1984). How many words are there in printed school English? *Reading Research Quarterly, 19*, 303–330.

Nagy, W. E., & Herman, P. A. (1987). Depth and breadth of vocabulary knowledge: Implications for acquisition and instruction. In M. G. McKeown & M. E. Curtis (Eds.), *The nature of vocabulary acquisition* (pp. 19–35). Hillsdale, NJ: Erlbaum.

National Reading Panel. (2000). *Teaching children to read: An evidence-based assessment of the scientific research literature on reading and its implications for reading instruction*. Washington, DC: U.S. Department of Health and Human Services.

*Stahl, S. A. (1999). *Vocabulary development*. Cambridge, MA: Brookline Books.

Stahl, S., & Fairbanks, M. (1986). The effect of vocabulary instruction: A model-based meta-analysis. *Review of Educational Research, 56,* 72–110.

White, T. G., Sowell, J., & Yanagihara, A. (1989). Teaching elementary students to use word-part clues. *The Reading Teacher, 42,* 302–308.

11 Direct Instruction of Comprehension Strategies

COMPETENCY 7.1
The reading professional will be able to provide direct instruction and model when and how to use multiple comprehension strategies, including retelling.

Interpretation

Comprehension strategies are defined as "specific procedures that guide students to become aware of how well they are comprehending as they attempt to read and write" (National Panel Report, 2000, p. 4-40). This competency appears to focus on both the **how** and the **what** of instruction in comprehension strategies. Because the competency begins with prescription for how comprehension strategies should be taught—through direct instruction and modeling—the main emphasis is probably on the method of instruction. Yet teachers are also asked to provide such instruction for "multiple comprehension strategies." With the exception of retelling, however, these strategies are not identified in this competency. Some comprehension strategies are included in other competencies (e.g., 7.2–7.6), but the IRA *Standards for Reading Professionals* does not specifically mention a number of comprehension strategies that are supported by research.

Because of our confusion about the main focus of Competency 7.1, we will discuss the prescribed instructional methods—direct instruction and modeling— and research-supported comprehension strategies that are not covered in other competencies.

Related Research

Research on Instructional Method

Competency 7.1 prescribes direct instruction and modeling when and how to use strategies. This approach, which has also been called "direct explanation" (Duffy et al., 1987) or "explicit instruction" (Pearson & Gallagher, 1983; Dole, Duffy, Roehler, & Pearson, 1991), is supported by research (National Reading Panel, 2000).

Direct instruction (to use the wording of the competency) includes three phases:

1. *Identifying, explaining, and modeling the strategy.* Teachers begin by defining what the strategy is. Then they explain why the students are learning the strategy (why it will be helpful to them in their reading), and when and where they should use the strategy. Next, the teacher models the strategy by explaining the thinking involved in using it. Through such "think alouds," teachers share with students the thought processes they use in performing the strategy, thus making the mental processes visible to the students.

2. *Guided practice.* During this phase, teachers require students to take more and more responsibility for the strategy until they are in control of the entire procedure. In shifting responsibility to the students, teachers provide some type of support (also called "scaffolding" to emphasize its temporary and adjustable nature) to help students follow the steps in the strategy as they work toward being able to perform the task independently. For example, teachers may provide hints and prompts to help students perform the task, and they may provide corrective feedback to help students understand what they did wrong and how they can correct it.

3. *Independent practice and application.* Finally, students are able to perform the strategy independently on new materials. In this phase, teachers still need to monitor student performance, reinstating scaffolding if needed.

Comprehension Strategies

This section will describe several comprehension strategies that have been identified from research about what works and what can be taught (e.g., Dole et al., 1991; National Reading Panel, 2000; Pearson & Fielding, 1991; Pressley, Johnson, Symons, McGoldrick, & Kurita, 1989). Most recently, the National Reading Panel identified 206 studies of comprehension that met their standards of scientific rigor. The Panel determined that seven individual strategies appeared "to be effective and most appropriate for classroom instruction" (2000, p. 4-44). The seven strategies identified by the Panel are comprehension monitoring, cooperative learning, graphic organizers, question answering, question generation, story structure, and summarization. Most of the strategies identified by the Panel agree with those identified in other sources; we believe, however, that cooperative learning is not a strategy, but rather a "pattern of classroom organization that allows students to work together to achieve their individual goals" (Harris & Hodges, 1995, p. 45). Therefore, cooperative learning is not a strategy in itself, but "a means for teaching a variety of comprehension strategies in small groups" (National Panel Report, 2000, p. 4-71). Therefore, we do not discuss cooperative learning in this chapter or other chapters related to comprehension strategies.

We include here those strategies mentioned by the National Reading Panel or by other sources and that are *not* covered in other competencies related to the category of comprehension (see Chapters 12, 13, 14, 15, and 19).

1. *Retelling.* We discuss this strategy first because it is the only strategy mentioned specifically in Competency 7.1. It is not, however, a comprehension strategy identified by the National Reading Panel or by most other resources we found. In retelling, children orally reconstruct stories that they have heard or read. Some research has shown that retelling is promising as a strategy for improving comprehension for kindergartners who are listening to stories as well as for older students reading stories. Apparently, even practice in retelling, without direct instruction, can facilitate comprehension (Gambrell, Koskinen, & Kapinus, 1991).

2. *Drawing inferences* (also called "inferencing"). Drawing inferences is essential to comprehension. Readers draw at least two kinds of inferences. First, they deduce relationships among the ideas in a text. For example, they may use information about a character in a story to determine the motives underlying the character's actions. A second way readers draw inferences is by using their prior knowledge (also called "background knowledge" or "world knowledge") to deduce what the text does not explicitly state. Examples of inferences that skilled readers make include filling in details omitted in the text, elaborating or going beyond given information in the text, and predicting what will happen next.

3. *Getting the main idea.* Effective comprehension depends on the ability to separate important from unimportant information. Skilled readers are able to determine the relative importance of information in a text. Researchers have determined that expert readers use at least three different methods to distinguish the relative importance of ideas in text. First, they use general background knowledge and prior knowledge of content to help them establish the meaning of a passage. Second, they use their knowledge of text structure to help them organize the information in a passage. This includes attending to textual features such as headings and subheadings, preview and summary statements, key words and phrases, and graphics. Third, proficient readers use their knowledge of author opinions, biases, purposes, and intentions to help them determine what is important.

4. *Summarizing.* Closely related to getting the main idea, or determining importance, is the ability to synthesize information across larger units of text to create summaries. Students must be able to integrate main ideas into a coherent summary that will presumably help them remember both important and supporting information about what they are reading. Creating a summary requires deleting irrelevant or redundant material, condensing information, locating topic sentences for paragraphs, and developing topic sentences for paragraphs that do not have them. Summarizing is thus a complex task that, even with instruction, develops gradually over time.

5. *Visualizing.* Comprehension and recall can be enhanced when readers visualize, or form mental images, of the text. Images can be representational, in which the reader visualizes the actual content of the text, such as a description of a burning village after a bombing. Another form of image is a mnemonic image, a reader-constructed image designed to aid memory. For example, in attempting to learn the attributes of a particular geographical region, students might construct a single mental image that includes a composite of all the attributes. Mnemonic imagery appears to be particularly useful when students must learn a large number of previously unknown concepts in a relatively short time.

What Does This Mean for You, the Teacher?

Some of your students have already acquired, or will be able to acquire, some or all of these comprehension strategies without much instruction. For example, even with less proficient students, retelling apparently improves simply with practice (Gambrell, Koskinen, & Kapinus, 1991). Also, practice in answering inference questions can enhance students' ability to draw inferences (Pearson & Fielding, 1991). For many strategies and many students, however, direct instruction will be required.

We recommend that you apply the general steps of direct instruction, as described in the "Related Research" section, to the teaching of *all* strategies. There is often no more effective way to teach comprehension strategies than to begin with modeling, using think-alouds and proceeding through the remaining steps of direct instruction. It is important to remember that you should always teach strategies in context when your students are attempting to comprehend actual classroom materials in order to accomplish particular learning tasks, such as writing answers to questions, performing a science experiment, or writing a report.

What follows are some additional suggestions for specific methods for teaching the comprehension strategies discussed in the section "Related Research."

1. *Retelling.* As previously mentioned, research has suggested that you can help your students simply by having them practice retelling. If your students have difficulty retelling stories, however, you can guide, or scaffold, the retelling by using the categories of a simplified story grammar: *setting, problem, goal, action, outcome.* You may also want your students to identify the *theme* of the story. For each category, use prompts or questions. For example, for the *setting,* you could ask Where did the story take place? When did the story take place? For the *action,* try the questions, What happened first? What happened next? For the *outcome,* How was the problem solved? or How did the main character achieve the goal? are good questions to ask. The *theme* could be prompted with a question, such as What do you think the author was trying to teach or tell you? When appropriate, you should also ask students to support their answers, using questions, such as Why do you think (a character) . . . did that?

2. *Drawing inferences.* Conventional wisdom seems to argue for delaying activities requiring inferences until students have become adept at lower-level, literal comprehension that does not require inferences. Research, however, clearly supports a strong emphasis on instruction in drawing inferences even in the earliest grades (Dole et al., 1991).

As previously mentioned, research suggests that one good way to help improve your students' ability to draw inferences is simply to ask them more questions that require inferences, with the provision of appropriate scaffolding.

Another way to improve inferencing is to teach students Question–Answer Relationships (QARs) (Raphael & Pearson, 1985; Raphael & Wonnacott, 1985). This method teaches students to determine when they can answer a question from the text alone, from their prior knowledge alone, or from a combination of prior knowledge and text information. Instruction in QARs has been shown to be especially helpful in answering questions requiring inferences. A description of this method is found in Raphael (1986).

3. *Getting the main idea.* Knowledge about the structure of text is important for helping readers differentiate important from less important information. One way you can help students determine the relative importance of ideas in text is to teach them the structures of narrative and expository texts. For narratives, use a story map with the categories of *setting, problem, goal, actions, outcome,* and, in most cases, *theme.* For expository text, you should teach students the structures of *enumeration, sequence* or *time order, comparison–contrast, cause–effect,* and *problem–solution.* The text structure defines the type of information that is most important for a given passage. For example, for an expository text with a *problem–solution* structure, the main ideas include the problem, the action taken to solve the problem, and the solution to the problem. One effective way to teach text structure is by using visual representations of the structures; these visual representations are sometimes called "maps." (See Johns & Lenski, 1997, for examples of maps for narrative and expository text structures.) Text structure is also discussed in Competencies 7.5 and 8.4.

Getting the main idea is closely related to the next strategy, summarizing. Determining importance is a necessary, but not a sufficient, condition for constructing a summary.

4. *Summarizing.* One way to help your students learn to summarize is to teach them to use text structure to guide their summaries. For example, for both narrative and expository text, you could begin by teaching them the text structure using a map, as suggested above. Then you could use a prompted paragraph format, also called a "frame," to help them construct the summary. A frame contains key words to prompt students to include important information in their summary of a particular text structure; there are different key words for each text structure. For example, a prompted paragraph, or frame, for a problem–solution structure might contain key words, such as "The problem was *(description of problem).* Therefore, *(action taken to solve problem).* As a result, *(solution to the problem)."* (Again, Johns & Lenski, 1997, provide examples of frames.)

Another approach you can use is to teach students to use the organizational features of a text to guide their construction of a "hierarchical summary" (e.g., Taylor & Beach, 1984; Taylor & Berkowitz, 1980). First, students use the headings, subheadings, and paragraphs to develop an outline of the text. They then develop main idea statements for every paragraph, subsection, and section of text and generate topic headings to connect sections of text. Finally, students generate a key idea to summarize the entire passage (see Taylor, 1982, for a full description of the procedure).

A third way you can teach your students to summarize is to use a set of basic rules developed and tested by researchers (e.g., Brown & Day, 1983; Rinehart, Stahl, & Erickson, 1986). The rules are: (1) delete trivial information, (2) delete redundant information, (3) substitute superordinate terms for members of a category (e.g., substitute sports for football, basketball, and baseball), (4) find and use any topic sentences or main ideas stated in the text, and (5) invent a topic sentence or main idea if the author has not provided one. Direct instruction in these rules can help students write better summaries.

5. *Visualizing.* To help students form representational images of text, encourage them to share the pictures that come to mind as they read descriptive text, asking them to point out words and phrases in the text that prompted their specific visual images. For younger students, you might ask them to draw pictures, perhaps in the form of a "visual response log" (Hubbard, Winterbourne, & Ostrow, 1996). For older students, you will probably also want to encourage verbal descriptions of visual imagery. Helping students form mnemonic images is more difficult, and we were unable to locate instructional guidelines. Providing direct instruction is the best advice we can offer.

In teaching your students all of these strategies, it is important to remember that direct instruction of strategies takes extended time and a great deal of practice. Ideally, instruction in comprehension strategies will take place throughout the school year and across the curriculum.

The report of the National Reading Panel suggests other implications for teachers. The Panel points out that many of these strategies fall into the category of "multiple strategies," and that the evidence supports the use of combinations of strategies in classroom reading instruction. Also, the Panel found substantial support for cooperative learning as a means for teaching a variety of comprehension strategies, especially in content areas and across the curriculum. Therefore, you might consider using some combination of direct instruction and cooperative learning to teaching comprehension strategies.

Summary

Competency 7.1 covers both method of instruction in comprehension strategies and type of comprehension strategies to teach. The chapter begins with an explanation of the research-supported method for teaching strategies—direct instruction. The chapter then identifies several specific reading comprehension strategies in addition to the single strategy of retelling that is mentioned in the competency. Finally, the chapter suggests ways of teaching each of the identified comprehension strategies.

REFERENCES

*Recommended for teachers

Braunger, J., & Lewis, J. P. (1997). *Building a knowledge base in reading*. Portland, OR: Northwest Regional Educational Laboratory.

Brown, A. L., & Day, J. D. (1983). Macrorules for summarizing texts: The development of expertise. *Journal of Verbal Learning and Verbal Behavior, 22*, 1–14.

Dole, J. A., Duffy, G. G., Roehler, L. R., & Pearson, P. D. (1991). Moving from the old to the new: Research on reading comprehension instruction. *Review of Educational Research, 61*(2), 239–264.

Duffy, G. G., Roehler, L. R., Sivan, E., Rackliffe, G., Book, C., Melkoth, M. S., Vavrus, L. G., Wesselman, R., Putnam, J., & Bassii, D. (1987). Effects of explaining the reasoning associated with using reading strategies. *Reading Research Quarterly, 23*(3), 347–368.

Gambrell, L. B., Koskinen, P. S., & Kapinus, B. A. (1991). Retelling and the reading comprehension of proficient and less-proficient readers. *Journal of Educational Research, 84*(6), 256–362.

Harris, T. L., & Hodges, R. E. (Eds.). (1995). *The literacy dicionary: The vocabulary of reading and writing*. Newark, DE: International Reading Association.

Hubbard, R. S., Winterbourne, N. W., & Ostrow, J. (1996). Visual responses to literature: Imagination through images. *The New Advocate, 9*(4), 309–323.

*Johns, J. L., & Lenski, S. D. (1997). *Improving reading: A handbook of strategies*. 2nd ed. Dubuque, IA: Kendall/Hunt.

National Reading Panel. (2000). *Teaching children to read: An evidence-based assessment of the scientific research literature on reading and its implications for reading instruction*. Washington, DC: National Institute of Child Health and Human Development.

Pearson, P. D., & Fielding, L. (1991). Comprehension instruction. In R. Barr, M. L. Kamil, P. Mosenthal, & P. D. Pearson. (Eds.). *Handbook of reading research*. Vol. II (pp. 815–860). White Plains, NY: Longman.

Pearson, P. D., & Gallagher, M. C. (1983). The instruction of reading comprehension. *Contemporary Educational Psychology, 8*, 317–344.

Pressley, M., Johnson, C. J., Symons, S., McGoldrick, J. A., & Kurita, J. A. (1989). Strategies that improve children's memory and comprehension of text. *The Elementary School Journal, 90*(1), 3–32.

*Raphael, T. E. (1986) Teaching question–answer relationships, revisited. *The Reading Teacher, 37*(6), 516–522.

Raphael, T. E., & Pearson, P. D. (1985). Increasing students' awareness of sources of information for answering questions. *American Educational Research Journal, 22*, 217–235.

Raphael, T. E., & Wonnacott, C. A. (1985). Heightening fourth-grade students' sensitivity to sources of information for answering questions. *Reading Research Quarterly, 20*, 282–296.

Rinehart, S. D., Stahl, S. A., & Erickson, L. G. (1986). Some effects of summarization training of reading and studying. *Reading Research Quarterly, 21*(4), 422–438.

*Taylor, B. M. (1982). A summarizing strategy to improve middle grade students' reading and writing skills. *The Reading Teacher, 20*, 202–205.

Taylor, B. M., & Beach, R. W. (1984). The effects of text structure instruction on middle-grade students' comprehension and production of expository text. *Reading Research Quarterly, 19*(2), 134–146.

Taylor, B. M., & Berkowitz, B. S. (1980). Facilitating children's comprehension of content material. In M. L. Kamil & A. J. Moe (Eds.), *Perspectives in reading research and instruction*. (Twenty-ninth Yearbook of the National Reading Conference, pp. 64–68.) Clemson, SC: National Reading Conference.

12 Questioning Strategies

COMPETENCY 7.2
Model questioning strategies.

Interpretation

The competency implies that teachers should use questioning strategies. Because all teachers use questioning strategies, we believe the competency as stated is not very informative. We think that the intention of the competency is much more profound: that teachers should both use *good* questioning strategies in their instruction and should also teach their students to use good questioning strategies, including self-questioning and answering questions. Therefore, we would reword the competency to say, "Use good questioning strategies in your instruction. In addition, teach your students how to generate good questions and how to answer questions well."

Related Research

This brief review of the massive body of research on questions and questioning will be organized around key questions most relevant to Competency 7.2.

Does Question-Asking Improve Student Learning?

Since classical Greek times, teachers' questions have been recognized as powerful forces in promoting learning. Questions have been described as "the single most influential teaching act" because of the power of questions to impact student thinking and learning (Taba, 1966, cited in Clegg, 1987, p. 13). Research supports that both oral teacher questions and written questions inserted in text (for example, questions at the ends of chapters) facilitate learning (Gall & Rhody, 1987). Also, more questions may be better than fewer questions (Rosenshine, 1986). Effective questions (1) keep students on task; (2) focus students' attention on what is to be learned; (3) elicit active, meaningful processing of the text; (4) activate metacognitive, or self-monitoring, processes; and (5) promote further practice and rehearsal of content.

What Types of Questions Are Most Effective?

One of the most thoroughly researched areas of questioning concerns the relative effectiveness of higher-cognitive versus lower-cognitive questions. The cognitive level of questions typically refers to Bloom's Taxonomy of Educational Objectives for the Cognitive Domain, with its ascending levels of knowledge, comprehension, application, analysis, synthesis, and evaluation. Higher-cognitive questions are usually defined as questions that require cognitive processes such as analysis, synthesis, evaluation, and problem-solving, while lower-cognitive questions require only memory of facts or the ability to find information in a source.

The research on this issue is surprisingly inconclusive. In one research review, Redfield and Rousseau (1981) concluded that teacher emphasis on higher-cognitive questions led to greater learning, but in another review of studies conducted in low-achieving urban schools, Rosenshine (1976) concluded that teachers' lower-cognitive questions were more effective in promoting academic achievement. Research on written questions in text, however, has found quite consistent results favoring higher-cognitive questions, at least for college-level students (Hamaker, 1986).

Should Questions Be Asked
Before, During, or After Reading?

Research has established that questions can be effective at all three phases of instruction—before, during, and after—but that the function of questions in each phase is different. Questions asked before reading can (1) help determine whether students have sufficient and accurate background knowledge about the topic of the reading, (2) help students access appropriate background knowledge that they possess but may not recognize as relevant, and (3) help students set a purpose for reading. For example, questions such as "What do you already know about _____?" and "What do you think will happen in the next part of the story based on what you already know?" can improve reading comprehension, particularly for poorer readers (Hansen & Pearson, 1983).

Questions asked during reading can play an important role in monitoring comprehension. During-reading questions should help students become aware of their comprehension failures and prompt the use of appropriate strategies for remediating those failures (see Chapter 14).

Questions asked after reading are most often used to assess student learning. Postreading questions can also play an important role in helping students review what they have read and to integrate the new information with their own background knowledge and experience.

What Is the Effect on Learning of Student-Generated Questions?

There is strong research evidence for the effectiveness of asking students to generate questions during reading (National Reading Panel, 2000). The act of composing questions encourages readers to be engaged in reading by requiring them to inspect the text carefully, focus on content, identify main ideas, and make connections among parts of the text and with their prior knowledge. Generating questions also fosters comprehension monitoring by helping students become aware of comprehension problems (Rosenshine, Meister, & Chapman, 1996).

It is not enough, however, simply to ask students to generate questions about what they are reading; they must be taught how to ask good questions. Many instructional studies designed to teach students to generate questions have resulted in improved text comprehension (Dole, Duffy, Roehler, & Pearson, 1991; Rosenshine, Meister, & Chapman, 1996). Most of these studies have used direct instruction to teach only the strategy of question generation. The approaches researchers have used include (1) teaching the key question-starting words (*who, what, when, where, why, how*); (2) teaching generic questions or question stems (e.g., *How does this passage relate to what I already know about the topic? How does _____ affect _____?*); (3) teaching students to compose questions based on main ideas; and (4) teaching students to use story grammar categories to generate questions.

Other studies have employed question generation as one strategy in a more comprehensive instructional package. Probably the best-known example is Reciprocal Teaching (Palincsar & Brown, 1984). In Reciprocal Teaching, students are taught four comprehension strategies—predicting, summarizing, clarifying, and asking questions. In the research studies on Reciprocal Teaching, question asking (and answering) appears to be the predominant strategy (Rosenshine, Meister, & Chapman, 1996). Other research-based instructional approaches in which student questioning plays a role include Questioning the Author (QtA) (Beck, McKeown, Hamilton, & Kucan, 1997) and the Book Club Project (McMahon, Raphael, Goatley, & Pardo, 1997).

What Techniques Help Students Give Good Answers to Questions?

One technique to help students give good answers to questions is to provide ample "wait time" (the time allowed by the teacher between asking a question and either receiving a response or repeating the question for someone else to answer). Rowe (1986) found that when teachers wait three seconds or more for a response, rather than the usual one second or less, important benefits include (1) increased length and quality of students' responses; (2) greater number of questions asked by students; (3) increased interaction with other students; (4) a wider range of students voluntarily participating; and (5) improved quality of subsequent written work related to the questioning. Teachers also benefit from wait time. Wait time encourages teachers to listen more carefully and thoughtfully to students' reasoning before reacting. Also, with increased wait time, teachers tend to ask more diverse questions.

A second way to help students answer questions well is to provide appropriate feedback to student responses. Researchers have identified two types of feedback: terminal feedback and sustaining feedback (Martin, Veldman, & Anderson, 1980). Terminal feedback occurs when the teacher immediately gives the desired answer or calls on another student to respond. Sustaining feedback includes restating questions, scaffolding the response by giving clues or prompts, and allowing ample time for students to respond (i.e., wait time). Research has shown that sustaining feedback promotes greater student achievement.

Instructional studies have revealed other techniques to help students answer questions well. One way is to teach students who may be experiencing difficulty in reading to look back in the text (i.e., reread) when they cannot answer a question after reading (Garner, Hare, Alexander, Haynes, & Winograd, 1984). Another instructional technique is to teach students where to find answers to questions. It is important for students to recognize that questions may be text-based, reader-based, or a combination of text- and reader-based, depending on the source of the answer. An instructional method called Question–Answer Relationship (QAR) (Raphael & Pearson, 1985; Raphael & Wonnacott, 1985) teaches students to determine when they can answer a question from the text alone, from their prior knowledge alone, or from a combination of prior knowledge and text information. Instruction in QARs has been shown to facilitate question answering in general and is especially helpful for questions requiring inferences. A description of this method is found in Raphael (1986).

What Does This Mean for You, the Teacher?

Because questions have a powerful effect on learning, it is important for teachers to ask good questions, to teach students how to ask good questions, and to elicit good responses. Here are some research-based suggestions for teaching students how to ask good questions:

1. Ask questions before, during, and after reading. Before reading, ask questions to determine what your students know about the topic of the selection they will read, for example, "What do you already know about _____?" Such questions will help your students begin to think about relevant knowledge and experience they already have. These questions will also help you determine whether you need to preteach any concepts critical to understanding the selection or whether your students have misconceptions that you need to address. Also ask before-reading questions to help your students set a purpose for reading, such as a question eliciting their prediction about the content of the text, for example, "What do you think the author will talk about in this section?" During reading, ask questions that encourage students to monitor their comprehension and take appropriate action if they are having problems with comprehension. For example, you might ask, "What does this mean?" "Is there anything unusual here?" "Is anyone still confused?" "Does this make sense with what was said previously?" "Who can summarize what's happened so far?" "What can we do to clarify that?" During reading you can also continue to ask your students to make predictions about what they will read next.

After reading, ask questions that help your students review what they have learned and engage in higher-order thinking, including connecting the new information with their prior knowledge. Examples of appropriate after-reading questions include "Were your predictions verified? Why or why not?" "Who can summarize what we've read?" "What conclusions can you draw about _____?" "Why is it important that _____?" "How does this passage relate to what we have learned before?" "How can you use this information in your everyday life?"

2. Ask thought-provoking questions. Use questioning to encourage and support higher-level thinking. One idea is to ask probing questions. Probing questions follow up on students' responses by asking them to rethink their answer, provide a more complete or adequate answer, or support the answer they gave. Probing questions encourage students to think at higher levels. Examples of probing questions are "Why do you say this?" "How do you know?" "Can you explain what you mean?" "Can you give an example?" "Can you explain how you came to that conclusion?"

3. Teach your students to ask their own good questions. Your modeling of good questioning strategies is the first step to helping your students become good self-questioners. As with any other strategy, your instruction should follow through with the rest of the steps of direct instruction (see Chapter 11). Of course, your students should learn how to ask questions about the content they are learning, but they should also learn to ask questions about the process they are using, comprehension-monitoring questions concerning their awareness and regulation of their own comprehension.

Fortunately, there are several available methods for helping students learn to ask questions. One popular method that encourages student questioning before, during, and after reading expository text is K-W-L (Ogle, 1986). K-W-L is an acronym for Know: What do I Know?, Want: What do I Want to Know?, and Learn: What have I Learned? K-W-L emphasizes students' prior knowledge, encourages them to ask questions, and directs them to seek answers to their questions. Other methods have already been mentioned in the section on "Related Research": Reciprocal Teaching, Questioning the Author, and the Book Club Project.

4. Help your students give good answers to questions. Be sure to provide a "wait time" of at least three seconds before reacting to student's responses. If students have answered inadequately, provide sustaining feedback by restating the question or giving clues or prompts. Also, by asking probing questions, you will elicit higher-level thinking (see [1] above). It will also be helpful if you teach students particular strategies for finding answers to questions. Depending on the level of your students, you may need to teach a strategy as simple as having them look back in the text to find answers. You can also teach students where to find answers to questions, perhaps by using the QAR method.

Summary

In summary, questioning can be a powerful strategy for enhancing students' learning. Research is generally supportive of asking higher-level, thought-provoking questions. Questions should be asked before, during, and after reading; they function differently in different positions. Students should be taught to generate their own questions, which can help them learn content as well as comprehension-monitoring strategies. Teachers can help students give better answers by providing ample wait time, appropriate feedback, and instruction on how to answer questions, such as teaching them where to find answers to questions. There is ample support for expanding Competency 7.2 to read, Use good questioning strategies in your instruction. In addition, teach your students how to generate good questions and how to answer questions well.

REFERENCES

*Recommended for teachers

*Beck, I. L., McKeown, M. G., Hamilton, R. L., & Kucan, L. (1997). *Questioning the author: An approach for enhancing student engagement with text*. Newark, DE: International Reading Association.

Clegg, A. A., Jr. (1987). Why questions? In W. W. Wilen (Ed.), *Questions, questioning techniques, and effective teaching* (pp. 11–22). Washington, DC: National Education Association.

Dole, J. A., Duffy, G. G., Roehler, L. R., & Pearson, P. D. (1991). Moving from the old to the new: Research on reading comprehension instruction. *Review of Educational Research, 61*(2), 239–264.

Gall, M. D., & Rhody, T. (1987). Review of research on questioning techniques. In W. W. Wilen (Ed.), *Questions, questioning techniques, and effective teaching* (pp. 23–48). Washington, DC: National Education Association.

Garner, R., Hare, V. C., Alexander, P., Haynes, J., & Winograd, P. (1984). Inducing use of a text lookback strategy among unsuccessful readers. *American Educational Research Journal, 21*, 789–798.

Hamaker, C. (1986). The effects of adjunct questions on prose learning. *Review of Educational Research, 56*, 212–242.

Hansen, J., & Pearson, P. D. (1983). An instructional study: Improving the inferential comprehension of fourth grade good and poor readers. *Journal of Educational Psychology, 75*, 821–829.

Martin, J., Veldman, D., & Anderson, L. M. (1980). Within-class relationships between student achievement and teacher behaviors. *American Educational Research Journal, 17*, 479–490.

*McMahon, S. I., Raphael, T. E., Goatley, V. J., & Pardo, L. S. (Eds.). (1997). *The Book Club connection: Literacy learning and classroom talk*. New York: Teachers College Press and Newark, DE: International Reading Association.

National Reading Panel. (2000). *Teaching children to read: An evidence-based assessment of the scientific research literature on reading and its implications for reading instruction.* Washington, DC: National Institute of Child Health and Human Development.

*Ogle, D. (1986). K-W-L: A teaching model that develops active reading of expository text. *The Reading Teacher, 39,* 564–570.

Palincsar, A. S., & Brown, A. L. (1984). Reciprocal teaching of comprehension-fostering and comprehension-monitoring activities. *Cognition and Instruction, 1,* 117–175.

*Raphael, T. E. (1986). Teaching question-answer relationships, revisited. *The Reading Teacher, 39,* 516–523.

Rapahel, T. E., & Pearson, P. D. (1985). Increasing students' awareness of sources of information for answering questions. *American Educational Research Journal, 22,* 217–235.

Raphael, T. E., & Wonnacott, C. A. (1985). Heightening fourth-grade students' sensitivity to sources of information for answering questions. *Reading Research Quarterly, 20,* 282–296.

Redfield, D. L., & Rousseau, E. W. (1981). A meta-analysis of experimental research on teacher questioning behavior. *Review of Educational Research, 51,* 237–245.

Rosenshine, B. V. (1976). Classroom instruction. In N. L. Gage (Ed.), *The psychology of teaching methods* (pp. 335–372). Chicago: University of Chicago Press.

Rosenshine, B. V. (1986). Synthesis of research on explicit teaching. *Educational Leadership, 43,* 60–69.

Rosenshine, B., Meister, C., & Chapman, S. (1996). Teaching students to generate questions: A review of the intervention studies. *Review of Educational Research, 66*(2), 181–221.

Rowe, M. B. (1986). Wait time: Slowing down may be a way of speeding up! *Journal of Teacher Education, 47,* 43–50.

13

Prior Knowledge

COMPETENCY 7.3
Teach students to connect prior knowledge with new information.

Interpretation

Prior knowledge, also called "background knowledge" or "world knowledge," is the existing store of knowledge that readers possess. (We prefer the term *background knowledge*, which we will use in this chapter.) Background knowledge includes knowledge about the world that individuals have accumulated through living. Reading is a process in which readers actively search for and construct meaning—comprehend—by relating what they are reading to their background knowledge.

We are puzzled by the wording of IRA Competency 7.3. Readers comprehend by connecting background knowledge to *all* information in a text, not just "new" information. We think the intent of the competency is probably "Help students comprehend text by drawing on their background knowledge."

One example of drawing on background knowledge is drawing inferences, one of the "multiple comprehension strategies" alluded to in Competency 7.1 and discussed in Chapter 11. We think the intent of Competency 7.3 is much broader than teaching inferencing, however. We believe it extends to any instruction that helps students draw on their background knowledge when reading. This includes instruction that facilitates students' ability to use background knowledge for specific selections that they read in the classroom as well as instruction that helps students learn how to make connections between their background knowledge and a text they are reading independently.

Related Research

One of the central theories of cognitive psychology that influences current thinking about reading is schema theory (Anderson & Pearson, 1984; Rumelhart, 1980). A schema is an organized structure in the mind in which an individual stores experiences and concepts. Schema theory explains how individuals acquire, store, and use knowledge. According to this theory, readers understand what they read only as it relates to what they already know. Readers construct meaning from text by connecting information in the text with their background knowledge. A great deal of research has demonstrated that background knowledge affects both the quality and the quantity of what is comprehended and remembered from reading (e.g., National Reading Panel, 2000).

Several types of background knowledge influence comprehension and memory:

1. General knowledge of the world, gained from accumulating life experiences. For example, knowledge of interpersonal relationships enables readers to interpret the actions of characters in stories.

2. Specific knowledge about various subjects. This is the particular information, including vocabulary, that is needed to understand a text about a specific topic. For example, a reader must know something about the game of chess (e.g., the names of pieces and moves and how the game is played) to understand an article reporting a chess match.

3. Knowledge about text. Readers need to know something about how texts work. For example, readers need to know about types of texts, or text genres—how fiction differs from nonfiction and how poetry differs from prose. Readers also need to understand the different organizational patterns of text. For example, readers need to know how stories and informational text are differently structured (see Chapters 15 and 19) and how novels differ from textbooks.

4. Strategic (or process) knowledge. Readers must also know *how* to read; that is, they must have decoding, comprehension, and metacomprehension strategies (see Chapters 7, 10, and 14).

Problems with background knowledge cause comprehension difficulties. Students may not have the prerequisite background knowledge; they may have it but fail to access it; they may have faulty or incompatible background knowledge; or, they may overrely on background knowledge and fail to use information from the text. These are all problems that can be addressed in instruction.

In summary, research emphasizes the crucial importance of background knowledge to reading comprehension and learning. Readers need general knowledge of the world, specific knowledge of the topic of the text, knowledge about text, and strategic knowledge about the reading process. Comprehension problems can occur if readers lack or fail to access background knowledge, if they have faulty or incompatible background knowledge, or if they overrely on background knowledge.

What Does This Mean for You, the Teacher?

You can help your students use background knowledge in reading in several ways and at different times: before, during, and after reading.

Before Reading

Prereading activities are especially important, as they prepare students to read a selection. Before students read, you should try to accomplish the following:

- *Activate background knowledge.* When you activate background knowledge, you help students recognize and use information they already possess. Your students probably possess some degree of knowledge about the text they are reading, but they may not think about what they know as they read. To activate background knowledge, you can ask students what they already know about the topic. You should be able to determine whether their background knowledge is adequate, inadequate, or erroneous (although, of course, this will vary from student to student).

- *Build background knowledge.* If you determine that your students' background knowledge is inadequate or erroneous, you will need to build knowledge by providing brief instruction on concepts that are critical to understanding the text. For example, if your students are about to read a selection about the Lewis and Clark Expedition, and their knowledge of relevant history and geography is weak, you can show them a map of the United States in the early nineteenth century, explain where North Americans were living at the time, and show them the Louisiana Territory, explaining that it was as yet unexplored.

- *Build text-specific knowledge.* Text-specific knowledge is more specific information about the reading selection, including key vocabulary and concepts, as well as information about the genre or organization of the text. One effective way to build text-specific knowledge is to provide students with a preview of the material they are going to read (Dole, Valencia, Greer, & Wardrop, 1991). The preview should contain information about key concepts and events of the text, perhaps including how the ideas will be organized and presented in the text. For example, you may provide students with an outline or graphic organizer of major concepts, showing their hierarchical organization.

- *Build vocabulary.* You may need to teach your students some key vocabulary words that they need to understand the text. Avoid the temptation to teach all words that you think may be unfamiliar to your students: Teach *only* those words that are critical to understanding the selection. If you attempt to teach your students all the new vocabulary before reading, they will not get the practice they need in acquiring vocabulary independently from reading. (For information on how to teach vocabulary, see Chapter 10.)

- *Set purposes and direction for reading.* Setting purposes for reading will help your students focus attention on what to look for as they read and help them connect their background knowledge with new information. One way to set purposes is to have your students ask questions about the text they will read, questions that they would like to find answered in the text. Another way of setting purposes is to ask students to make predictions about the text and then read to confirm or disconfirm their predictions. Of course, both the questions students ask and the predictions they make are based on their background knowledge (including any background knowledge building you have already done with them).

Direction-setting should occur at the end of your prereading activities. You may want to give your students a final word of guidance about what to attend to while they read. For example, you might say, "Read the chapter to see if you can find answers to your questions" or "Read the selection to find out whether your predictions are correct." In some cases, especially for relatively difficult informational text, you may wish to prepare a reading guide, which may consist of questions to answer or graphic organizers or outlines to complete.

■ *Suggest comprehension strategies.* Before your students read, it is also important to remind them to use the comprehension strategies you have taught them. (See the other chapters in this section on comprehension.) For example, you might say, "As you read, try to summarize each section in your head" or "Remember to ask yourself if what you're reading is making sense to you, and if it isn't, try rereading the section" or "Try to create a picture in your imagination of what's happening as you read this chapter."

During Reading

During-reading activities should facilitate or enhance students' reading comprehension during the actual reading process. Probably the most common way that teachers attempt to enhance comprehension during reading is through questioning. Questions can help students understand the selection and help teachers discover how well they understand it. Good questions will provide students with the opportunity to organize and integrate information, to see important connections and relationships they might otherwise miss. Good questions can also help readers see the relationship between what they are reading and what they already know. (Chapter 12 provides guidelines for how to ask good questions.)

You can also help your students engage in a number of other helpful activities as they read. Some possibilities follow. Of course, you will not want to do *all* of these activities with a single text; select one or two activities that are most useful for the given text and for your teaching purposes.

■ Have your students follow through on the prereading purpose-setting activities, for example, trying to find answers to questions they posed or confirming or disconfirming predictions they made.

■ Continue to remind your students to use some of the comprehension strategies you suggested before they began reading.

■ Encourage your students to make inferences, draw conclusions, or predict outcomes.

■ Remind your students to complete the reading guide as they read, if you have prepared one.

■ Ask your students to record main ideas and supporting details, outline, summarize, and make graphic organizers.

- Ask your students to record their responses in journals or engage in other informal writing activities, such as note taking, as they read.
- Ask your students to read with a partner or in a small group, pausing to reflect on and discuss what they are reading.

After Reading

Postreading activities should help students *do* something with what they have just read in order to tighten the connection between their background knowledge and information in the text. You can encourage them to think critically and creatively about what they have read and to apply and extend their new learnings. The following are suggestions for helpful postreading activities.

- *Further questioning.* Postreading questions should help students apply, analyze, synthesize, or elaborate the information and ideas in the material they have read, either orally or in writing. Such questions should include a follow-up to the questions that were asked in the prereading and during-reading stages. Postreading questions can be posed by both teachers and students.
- *Discussion.* The purpose of discussion is for students to exchange ideas freely in order to gain new understandings or perspectives. Research has shown that small-group discussions about texts can enhance comprehension and recall as well as personal connection to the text (Gambrell, 1996). (*Discussion* is further discussed later in this section and in Chapter 2.)
- *Writing.* Because writing requires the active manipulation of ideas, it is a powerful way to help your students connect what they already know with new information in the text. Many forms of writing are possible, for example, summaries, journals, reports, letters, poems, stories, and so on. Of course, the writing should relate to the purpose for reading.
- *Drama, art, music, and dance.* Drama, art, music, and dance are other ways that your students can respond to what they have read in order to facilitate the connection between background knowledge and new information. Such activities may be particularly helpful to learners who are not predominantly verbal but who can enhance or demonstrate their knowledge and understanding in alternative expressive forms.
- *Application and outreach in the real world.* These activities can be especially helpful for strengthening the connection between background knowledge and reading. Applications may be as simple as actually doing something described in a text, such as following directions for how to conduct an experiment or make a certain kind of map. Applications may also entail major projects that extend to the community. For example, after reading a chapter on pollution, students could organize a community campaign to identify and solve local problems with pollution.

In addition to the specific activities that you can use before, during, and after reading that are described in this section, several integrated procedures have been developed that include before-, during-, and after-reading activities. Probably the most well known and frequently used procedure, especially with informational text, is K-W-L (Ogle, 1986). (Also see Chapter 12.) K-W-L stands for What do you Know? What do you Want to Know? And What did you Learn? The three phases of the procedure correspond to the before-, during-, and after-reading stages and reinforce students' active involvement in connecting background knowledge with new information.

The Directed Reading–Thinking Activity, or DR–TA, is another procedure that takes students through the before, during, and after stages of reading (Stauffer, 1969). In DR–TA, teachers have students make their own predictions about what they are about to read, read to confirm or disconfirm their predictions, and support their conclusion about the validity of their predictions by referring to the passage that contains the information. A second, skill-based phase occurs after the directed-thinking phase. This phase can involve postreading activities, such as vocabulary study or summarizing, which require the students to reexamine the text.

Inquiry Charts, or I-Charts (Hoffman, 1992) were developed to foster critical thinking by having students gather information from several sources and organize it for summarization, comparison, and evaluation. Students explore their background knowledge concerning several questions about a topic; read and record information on the I-Chart from different sources in response to the questions; generate summary statements in response to each question; compare the information gained from their readings with their background knowledge and reconcile any discrepancies. Students also investigate additional questions that have arisen during their reading. Finally, they can expand their summaries into paragraphs or full reports.

Other methods also involve the active involvement of students in discussion throughout the reading process. A few examples of such discussion methods are the Shared Inquiry approach of the Great Books Foundation (1992), Questioning the Author (QtA) (Beck, McKeown, Hamilton, & Kucan, 1997), and the Book Club Project (McMahon, Raphael, Goatley, & Pardo, 1997). (These methods are also discussed more extensively in Chapters 12 and 15.)

Although the before-, during-, and after-reading activities discussed in this section are teacher-directed, it is obviously important for students to internalize the strategies involved. Repeated engagement in the types of activities recommended here should help students learn why, when, where, and how to use such strategies to help them connect their background knowledge with texts they read independently.

Summary

Connecting background knowledge to texts is essential for comprehension and learning, so it is vital for reading professionals to help students make this connection. This chapter has focused on ways that teachers can facilitate the background knowledge–text connection for particular reading selections before, during, and after reading. Several integrated procedures that entail making connections throughout the reading process were also presented. Another aspect of connecting background knowledge to information in texts is making inferences, one of the comprehension strategies discussed in Chapter 11.

REFERENCES

*Recommended for teachers

Anderson, R. C., & Pearson, P. D. (1984). A schema-theoretic view of reading comprehension. In P. D. Pearson (Ed.), *Handbook of reading research* (pp. 255–291). New York: Longman.

*Beck, I. L., McKeown, M. G., Hamilton, R. L., & Kucan, L. (1997). *Questioning the author: An approach for enhancing student engagement with text.* Newark, DE: International Reading Association.

Dole, J. A., Valencia, S. W., Greer, E. A., & Wardrop, J. L. (1991). Effects of two types of prereading instruction on the comprehension of narrative and expository text. *Reading Research Quarterly, 26,* 142–159.

Great Books Foundation. (1992). *An introduction to shared inquiry,* 3rd ed. Chicago, IL: Great Books Foundation.

*Hoffman, J. V. (1992). Critical reading/thinking across the curriculum: Using I-charts to support learning. *Language Arts, 69,* 121–127.

*McMahon, S. I., Raphael, T. E., Goatley, V. J., & Pardo, L. S. (Eds.). (1997). *The Book Club connection: Literacy learning and classroom talk.* New York: Teachers College Press and Newark, DE: International Reading Association.

National Reading Panel. (2000). *Teaching children to read: An evidence-based assessment of the scientific research literature on reading and its implications for reading instruction.* Washington, DC: National Institute of Child Health and Human Development.

*Ogle, D. (1986). K-W-L: A teaching model that develops active reading of expository text. *The Reading Teacher, 39,* 564–570.

Rumelhart, D. E. (1980). Schemata: The building blocks of cognition. In R. J. Spiro, B. C. Bruce, & W. F. Brewer (Eds.), *Theoretical issues in reading comprehension* (pp. 33–58). Hillsdale, NJ: Erlbaum.

Stauffer, R. G. (1969). *Directing reading maturity as a cognitive process.* New York: Harper & Row.

14 Monitoring Comprehension

COMPETENCY 7.4
Teach students strategies for monitoring their own comprehension.

Interpretation

"Comprehension monitoring in the act of reading is the noting of one's successes and failures in developing or attaining meaning, usually with reference to an emerging conception of the meaning of the text as a whole, and adjusting one's reading process accordingly" (Harris & Hodges, 1995, p. 39). It is important to recognize that comprehension monitoring consists of two parts: being aware of the quality and extent of one's understanding of text, and, when comprehension fails, knowing what to do and how to do it. These two aspects have been referred to as "knowledge and control," "awareness and regulation," or "self-appraisal and self-management" (Paris, Wasik, & Turner, 1991).

Related Research

Considerable research has established that older and more proficient readers are better than younger and less proficient readers at monitoring, controlling, and adapting their strategic reading processes. Older and more proficient readers are more aware of problems that arise during reading and are more able to solve these problems (Dole, Duffy, Roehler, & Pearson, 1991; Garner, 1987; Paris, Wasik, & Turner, 1991). Among the strategies that skilled readers use to remediate comprehension problems—also called "fix-up strategies"—are the following: (1) rereading, reading the text again in order to discover information that might have been missed on the first reading; (2) reading ahead to search for additional information that might clarify the comprehension problem; (3) using other comprehension strategies, such as visualizing or using context clues; and (4) seeking help from another source, such as a reference book or a teacher.

A good deal of instructional research has shown that children in grades two through six can be taught to monitor their comprehension, to become aware of problems in comprehension, and to learn procedures to assist them in overcoming the problem (National Reading Panel, 2000). Even very young children can learn, through direct instruction, to be aware of whether something they read makes sense or not (Paris, Wasik, & Turner, 1991). Older children can learn more sophisticated forms of comprehension monitoring. We present just a few examples of instruction that have been shown to be successful in promoting comprehension monitoring in older children.

Paris, Cross, and Lipson (1984) taught third and fifth graders several comprehension strategies that involved extensive discussion using metaphorical prompts such as "Be a reading detective" and "Plan your reading trip," as well as practice with feedback and application in content areas. After about thirty hours of instruction, students exhibited significant increases in their awareness about reading, comprehension monitoring, and strategic reading.

Baumann, Jones, and Seifert-Kessell (1993) taught fourth graders a variety of comprehension and comprehension-monitoring strategies, including asking questions; drawing on prior knowledge; asking themselves, "Is this making sense?"; predicting and verifying; drawing inferences; retelling; and rereading and reading on to clarify meaning. In a series of ten lessons, the teachers modeled the strategies using think-alouds and then had students use think-alouds as they applied the strategies while reading. Think-alouds were found to be an effective tool for helping students acquire a number of comprehension and comprehension-monitoring strategies.

Palincsar and Brown (1984) developed a method called "Reciprocal Teaching," which combines the four strategies of predicting, asking important questions, clarifying unclear segments, and summarizing. Students first learn each strategy with the help of an adult teacher or peer tutor (Palincsar, Brown, & Martin, 1987) in a collaborative learning format. Then students take turns acting as teachers and students in group reading activities involving the four strategies, with the adult teacher or peer tutor providing guidance, feedback, and elaboration. Reciprocal Teaching has been shown to be an effective method to help students of all abilities from ages five to fifteen gain awareness and regulation of their reading comprehension (Palincsar, Brown, & Martin, 1987). Reciprocal Teaching does, however, require a great deal of instructional time.

Another successful example of an approach to teaching comprehension strategies, including comprehension monitoring, is "transactional strategies instruction," a general approach to instruction that has been shown to be successful in many classrooms (Pressley, 1998; Pressley, et al., 1992). In transactional strategies instruction, a wide variety of comprehension and interpretation strategies are taught through direct instruction and practiced by students working with the teacher in collaborative groups. Transactional strategies instruction occurs throughout the school year and often across the curriculum.

A final example of an approach to comprehension instruction (including comprehension monitoring) that involves collaborative discussion is "Questioning the Author" (QtA) (Beck, McKeown, Hamilton, & Kucan, 1997). A key feature of QtA is that students grapple with meaning *during* reading instead of discussing questions *after* reading. Teachers initiate and sustain discussion during reading through the use of carefully designed "queries," or probes that focus on meaning, and "discussion moves," which are actions the teacher takes to keep students engaged in constructing an understanding of the text. QtA has been successful at fostering comprehension and comprehension monitoring in many elementary classrooms when applied over extended time.

In summary, considerable evidence exists that instruction can help students become better at monitoring their reading comprehension. Generally, teaching comprehension-monitoring strategies requires instruction over an extended period of time, and comprehension monitoring is often taught in conjunction with other comprehension strategies.

What Does This Mean for You, the Teacher?

Because comprehension monitoring is a critical attribute of skilled readers, you will want to provide instruction that encourages students to monitor their comprehension as they read. Your instruction should include both aspects of comprehension monitoring by helping your students to evaluate their comprehension while reading and to take remedial action if comprehension fails. Be sure to teach students a variety of fix-up strategies, including rereading, reading ahead, using other comprehension strategies, and consulting other resources.

As with teaching any strategy, you should first explain *what* comprehension monitoring is, *why* it is important and how monitoring can make your students better readers, and *when* they should apply the strategy. Next, you should teach your students *how* to monitor their comprehension by following the direct instruction model. We recommend that you begin by modeling your own comprehension monitoring through thinking aloud as you read a short text segment that is somewhat challenging (for example, one that contains ambiguities, unclear referents, unfamiliar vocabulary, difficult concepts). Be sure to model both your awareness or knowledge of your own comprehension and the strategies you might use to resolve comprehension problems.

You may also want to use one of the methods discussed in the "Related Research" section. Baumann, Jones, and Seifert-Kessell's (1993) instruction in using think-alouds and Beck, McKeown, Hamilton, and Kucan's (1997) QtA approach, although quite different, are both explained clearly and comprehensively for classroom teachers.

Summary

In summary, research supports comprehension monitoring as a critical strategy for skilled reading. Comprehension monitoring includes both an awareness of the quality and extent of one's understanding of a text, and a knowledge of what to do when comprehension breaks down. Instruction in comprehension monitoring can be effective, but it requires considerable classroom time.

REFERENCES

*Recommended for teachers

*Baumann, J. F., Jones, L. A., & Seifert-Kessell, N. (1993). Using think alouds to enhance children's comprehension monitoring abilities. *The Reading Teacher, 47*(3), 184–193.

*Beck, I. L., McKeown, M. G., Hamilton, R. L., & Kucan, L. (1997). *Questioning the author: An approach for enhancing student engagement with text.* Newark, DE: International Reading Association.

Dole, J. A., Duffy, G. G., Roehler, L. R., & Pearson, P. D. (1991). Moving from the old to the new: Research on reading comprehension instruction. *Review of Educational Research, 61*(2), 239–264.

Garner, R. (1987). *Metacognition and reading comprehension.* Norwood, NJ: Ablex.

Harris, T. L., & Hodges, E. (Eds.). (1995). *The literacy dictionary: The vocabulary of reading and writing.* Newark, DE: International Reading Association.

National Reading Panel. (2000). *Teaching children to read: An evidence-based assessment of the scientific research literature on reading and its implications for reading instruction.* Washington, DC: National Institute of Child Health and Human Development.

Palincsar, A. S., & Brown, A. (1984). Reciprocal teaching of comprehension-fostering and comprehension-monitoring activities. *Cognition and Instruction, 1*, 117–175.

Palincsar, A. S., Brown, A. L., & Martin, S. M. (1987). Peer interaction in reading comprehension instruction. *Educational Psychologist, 22*, 231–253.

*Paris, S. G., Cross, D. R., & Lipson, M. Y. (1984). Informed strategies for learning: A program to improve children's reading awareness and comprehension. *Journal of Educational Psychology, 76*, 1239–1252.

Paris, S. G., Wasik, B. A., & Turner, J. C. (1991). The development of strategic readers. In R. Barr, M. L. Kamil, P. Mosenthal, & P. D. Pearson (Eds.), *Handbook of reading research*, Vol. II (pp. 609–640). New York: Longman.

Pressley, M. (1998). Comprehension strategies instruction. In J. Osborn, & F. Lehr, (Eds.), *Literacy for all: Issues in teaching and learning* (pp. 113–133). New York: Guilford.

Pressley, M., El-Dinary, P. B., Gaskins, I., Schuder, T., Berman, J. L., Almasi, J., & Brown, R. (1992). Beyond direct explanation: Transactional instruction of reading comprehension strategies. *The Elementary School Journal, 92*(3), 513–555.

15 Aspects of Text

COMPETENCY 7.5
Ensure that students can use various aspects of text to gain comprehension, including conventions of written English, text structure and genres, figurative language, and intertextual links.

COMPETENCY 7.6
Ensure that students gain understanding of the meaning and importance of the conventions of standard written English (e.g., punctuation or usage).

Interpretation

We grouped these competencies together because they seem redundant to us. Competency 7.5 mentions "conventions of written English" as one of five aspects of text, while Competency 7.6 focuses exclusively on conventions of written English, modified by the adjective "standard."

Competency 7.5 implies that teachers should teach students how to use five quite different aspects of text in order to help them comprehend a text. The first text aspect, *conventions of written English*, is somewhat ambiguous. Competency 7.6 provides two examples of conventions of standard written English: punctuation or usage. According to an IRA/NCTE publication, *Standards for the English Language Arts* (1996), conventions of written English include grammar, punctuation, and spelling. We will adopt the latter, more complete, definition of English conventions.

The second aspect of text listed in Competency 7.5 is *text structure*. Text structure refers to the underlying organizational pattern of a text. Narratives (stories) have a different structure than informational text, and informational text is organized in various ways. The structures of narratives and informational texts have been identified and defined.

The third aspect of text mentioned in Competency 7.5 is *genre*, a French word meaning "type" or "kind." Although *genre* has varying definitions, we believe that in this competency *genre* probably refers to literary genres, or categories of children's literature based on type of content. All literature is either poetry or prose. Prose is further divided into fiction and nonfiction. Fiction includes fantasy (traditional, modern, and science fiction) and realism (historical fiction and contemporary realistic fiction). Nonfiction includes biography and informational books. Some sources also identify picture books and multicultural literature as separate genres.

Figurative language includes similes, metaphors, and personification. Similes compare two different things using *like* or *as*. Metaphors compare two different things without using a word of comparison such as *like* or *as*. In personification, an idea, object, or animal is given the characteristics of a person.

Intertextual links should not be confused with *intertextuality*, which is simply defined as the reader's construction of meaningful connections among texts they have read (e.g., Bloome & Egan-Robertson, 1993). Because *intertextuality* refers to a process carried out in the mind of the reader, it is not an aspect of text. Therefore, intertextuality cannot be the same as the intertextual links referred to in Competency 7.5. Our interpretation is that intertextual links are cues in a text that remind the reader of other texts. For example, "Once upon a time . . ." will signal to most readers that the upcoming text will be a folktale similar to many other folktales they know that begin with the same phrase.

*Intra*textual links were not mentioned in the competency, but this aspect of text certainly affects comprehension. Intratextual links provide cohesion among the various propositions of the text. In other words, they are the glue that binds the various parts of a text together. Some examples of intratextual links are references from one part of the text to another (for example, pronoun references or phrases such as "as previously mentioned," or "see Chapter 5"), signaling devices that designate particular text structures (such as "On the one hand . . . on the other hand," or "First, second, third . . ."), transition phrases and sentences, and overviews or summaries.

Related Research

In this section we will discuss the research related to each of the five aspects of text mentioned in the two competencies.

Conventions of Written English

The literature on reading comprehension with which we are familiar does not mention knowledge of the conventions of written English. Also, a computer search failed to yield any research showing a direct relationship between knowledge of conventions of written English and comprehension. Comprehension, however, depends on fast and accurate word identification, so perhaps research linking conventions of written English to word identification is relevant here. In Chapter 6 we discussed the role of one aspect of grammar, syntax, and in Chapter 9 we discussed the role of spelling, a graphophonic cue, in word identification.

We could find no research regarding the role of punctuation or capitalization in comprehension. Nonetheless, it makes sense that students must learn to utilize punctuation in order to become fluent readers. For example, when they read aloud, beginning readers need to learn to pause slightly at commas and longer at periods. What is not known is how the ability to use punctuation and capitalization in oral reading affects comprehension. Of course, knowledge of the conventions of written English is important in writing, but we frankly do not understand the IRA's emphasis—in two competencies—on written English conventions as aids to reading comprehension.

Text Structure

Research has established a strong relationship between the reader's understanding of the organization, or structure, of texts, and reading comprehension. As discussed in Chapter 19, research has established that (1) the more students are aware of and strategically use text organization, the better their comprehension; and (2) explicit instruction in text organization facilitates comprehension (e.g., Dickson, Simmons, & Kameenui, 1995). A well-established research basis exists for the recommendation that students use knowledge of text structure to enhance their comprehension.

Genres

We were unable to locate any research showing a relationship between knowledge of specific literary genres and reading comprehension. It seems logical, however, that if readers know what literary genre they are about to read, they know what to expect from the text, for example, a moral in a fable or facts about a person's life in a biography. And that expectation is likely to help them construct meaning and comprehend the text. So, even if research does not directly support teaching about specific genres, common sense suggests that knowledge of the characteristics of different genres will be helpful to students.

Figurative Language

Again, while we could locate no research directly linking knowledge of figurative language with reading comprehension, it is reasonable to assume that students' ability to interpret figurative language will affect their comprehension. A student who does not understand the intent of similes, metaphors, and personification is likely to be stymied by a text that uses these forms of figurative language to convey meaning.

Intertextual Links

Our confusion about the meaning of intertextual links may have impeded our ability to search for relevant research. We were, however, unable to find any literature that clarified the meaning of intertextual links in text or that described research supporting the role of intertextual links in comprehension.

What Does This Mean for You, the Teacher?

Competencies 7.5 and 7.6 encourage you to teach your students about various aspects of text that are likely to help them understand what they are reading. We believe some aspects are more helpful than others, and that will be reflected in our recommendations. Our top candidate for a useful aspect of text to teach students is text structure, primarily because there is a good deal of research showing the effectiveness of instruction in text structure on comprehension. Chapter 19 discusses several ideas for how you might teach text structure.

In addition to direct teaching of text structure and in keeping with the recommendations of other competencies, you should encourage your students to engage in wide reading of a variety of texts. As you introduce students to different types, or genres, of texts, it makes sense to teach them about the defining characteristics of each genre. For example, if you were to use Patricia MacLachlan's novel *Sarah, Plain and Tall* in teaching about pioneer life on the prairie, you might tell students that, in historical fiction, writers try to tell stories that show how living in a particular time and place influenced the lives of people, especially ordinary people. By reading *Sarah, Plain and Tall*, students can gain a sense of what it might have been like to live on the Midwest prairie during the mid to late 1800s. Classifying genres can sometimes be difficult because many books represent more than one genre. For example, Paul Fleischman's *Joyful Noise: Poems for Two Voices* is poetry, but it also conveys facts about insects and, therefore, is in some sense nonfiction (informational text) as well.

While your students are reading widely, it also makes good sense to teach them about figurative language as it occurs in the texts they are reading. Poetry, of course, is a good genre to use in introducing figurative language. The poem by Georgia Heard, "Compass," provides an opportunity to teach personification, metaphor, and simile. The compass is personified as a skater, in one place by using the simile "like a skater." Metaphors are used to describe the compass.

Of course, other genres besides poetry include figurative language. For example, you can point out to your students that a metaphor is being used when the United States is described as a "melting pot" in their social studies textbook. In addition to your regular classroom reading materials, you can find suggestions for resources to use in teaching particular types of figurative language in library reference materials and some textbooks about children's literature.

Competency 7.5 may have intended to include the closely related language form of idioms in the category of figurative language. Idioms are forms of speech, or expressions, that are used in a peculiar way in a given language. By definition, idioms, for example, "passing the buck," "putting one's foot down," and "chip on one's shoulder," cannot be interpreted literally. You will need to teach your students what unfamiliar idioms really mean, which is probably best accomplished within the context in which they appear in classroom reading materials. Prevalent in both spoken and written English, idioms often pose comprehension problems, especially for children whose first language is not English.

If you are a primary grade teacher, you will want to teach conventions of written English as you teach your students to read. We recommend teaching the conventions as they occur in the materials students read in your classroom. For example, consider punctuation. You will probably begin by teaching your students about sentences ending with a period, indicating that they should pause in their oral reading. Then, as question marks and exclamation marks occur, you can help your students learn about those forms of ending punctuation and how they affect inflection in their oral reading. When quotation marks appear in students' reading material, you will want to teach the significance of those marks. Similarly, you can point out spelling patterns and aspects of grammar as they appear in classroom reading materials.

Of course, you will also want to help your students learn to use the conventions of written English as they write (see Chapter 21). Help your students see the relationships between the conventions used in the texts they are reading and the personal text they are attempting to write.

We have no recommendations to offer concerning teaching about intertextual links because we are unclear about what these are. Regarding intratextual links, however, we do have some very specific suggestions. Understanding intratextual links requires making inferences, one of the key comprehension strategies discussed in Chapter 10. For example, consider Ryan Oba's short story "Home Now," which begins "It was five in the afternoon, and already the sun was going down. A jackknifed trailer two miles ahead had traffic backed up to where Robert's Honda was—stuck under an underpass, surrounded by other cars." Two paragraphs later, with no further mention of the traffic snarl, is the statement, "there was no sign of this jam being cleared up in the near future" (p. 45). Readers have to make the inference that "this jam" (an intratextual link) refers to the traffic snarl described two paragraphs earlier.

In your classroom reading materials, you can select examples of different kinds of intratextual links to use in your direct instruction of inferencing. As suggested in Chapter 10, your instruction on making inferences about intratextual links may focus on asking questions about these links or teaching students question-answer relationships (QARs) involving intratextual links.

In addition to intratextual links, there are other aspects of text not mentioned in Competencies 7.5 and 7.6 that we believe you should teach. In particular, students need instruction regarding how to read informational text, especially their content area textbooks. We recommend teaching students how to use tables of content, indexes, and glossaries. Teach your students about the function of headings and subheadings in text. Tell your students about the importance of reading overviews and summaries of chapters and sections. Encourage them to examine graphics (photographs, drawings, diagrams, graphs, maps, etc.), to read their accompanying captions, and to think about the relationship of the graphics to the information in the text. Help your students take advantage of any special features a particular publisher might include, such as graphic organizers or special advice to aid the reader.

Summary

Competencies 7.5 and 7.6 prescribe teaching particular aspects of text—conventions of written English, text structure, genres, figurative language, and intertextual links—

as aids to comprehension. Although common sense supports teaching most of these aspects of text, there is really only strong research support for teaching text structure. The aspect of conventions of written English is mentioned in Competency 7.5 and is the exclusive focus of Competency 7.6, yet we cannot agree that knowledge of conventions plays a prominent role in reading comprehension, except perhaps at the beginning reading level. We are also puzzled by the inclusion of intertextual links rather than intratextual links. Finally, we believe Competency 7.5 omits other important aspects of text, particularly the special text features of content area textbooks, that we believe students should know in order to facilitate their ability to read and learn from texts.

REFERENCES

International Reading Association and National Council of Teachers of English. (1996). *Standards for the English language arts*. Newark, DE and Urbana, IL: Author.

Bloome, D., & Egan-Robertson, A. (1993). The social construction of intertextuality in classroom reading and writing lessons. *Reading Research Quarterly, 28*(4), 304–333.

Dickson, S. V., Simmons, D. C., & Kameenui, E. J. (1995). *Text organization and its relation to reading comprehension: A synthesis of the research*. (Tech. Rep. No. 17). Eugene, OR: University of Oregon, National Center to Improve the Tools of Educators.

Fleischman, P. (1988). *Joyful noise: Poems for two voices*. New York: Harper & Row.

Heard, G. (1999). Compass. In L. B. Hopkins (Ed.), *School supplies: A book of poems*. New York: Simon & Schuster.

MacLachlan, S. (1985). *Sarah, plain and tall*. New York: Harper & Row.

Oba, R. (1998, September/October). Home now. *Cicada 1*(1), 45–51.

16 Multiple Sources

COMPETENCY 8.1
Provide opportunities to locate and use a variety of print, nonprint, and electronic reference sources.

Interpretation

Given the exponential growth in both the amount and variety of information resources in the "Information Age," it is especially important that students learn to handle and use information in efficient and effective ways. Competency 8.1 alludes to the importance of what others have called "information literacy"—the ability to access, evaluate, organize, and use information from a variety of sources (Breivik & Ford, 1993; Carr, 1999; Humes, 1999). Those who are information literate "know how to learn because they know how knowledge is organized, how to find information, and how to use information in such a way that others can learn from them" (American Library Association, 1989, p. 2). Learning how to learn is fundamental to economic and personal success. The U.S. Department of Labor Secretary's Commission on Achieving Necessary Skills (SCANS) includes information literacy as one of the five essential competencies needed for successful job performance (Humes, 1999). Information literacy is critical for effective problem-solving and decision making, freedom of choice, and full participation in a democratic society.

It is significant to note, however, that Competency 8.1 recommends simply "providing opportunities" for locating and using a variety of sources; it does not specifically recommend teaching the skills and strategies essential to information literacy.

Related Research

In information literacy, the emphasis shifts from students *having* information to *using* information to construct their own learning. The student's active role in learning is supported by research in cognitive science, which recognizes that the process of accessing, evaluating, and using information is integral to understanding content (Carr, 1999).

An emphasis on information literacy has profound implications for teaching. In order for students to become information literate, they must assume responsibility for gaining knowledge. Students have to be able to pose questions, develop strategies to search for answers, and formulate conclusions. The role of the teacher, therefore, becomes that of a coach or guide rather than the disseminator of information. Teachers need to help students learn how to become active participants in the learning process by encouraging learner-based inquiry and the scientific inquiry process (Humes, 1999).

Unfortunately, little progress has been made in implementing the teaching of information literacy in schools. In the 1989 report issued by the American Library Association Presidential Committee on Information Literacy, one of six recommendations made was: "Teacher education and performance expectations should be modified to include information literacy concerns." A 1998 update of this report (infolit.org/documents/progress.html) concluded that *no* progress had been made on this recommendation in the intervening nine years. In other words, few programs of teacher education have information literacy requirements and few states require teachers to demonstrate competency in teaching information literacy.

What Does This Mean for You, the Teacher?

Given the state of the art of information literacy research and development, it is probably fortunate that this competency does not expect you to *teach* information literacy. Rather, you are simply asked to "provide opportunities" for students to locate and use a variety of reference sources. Obviously, you need to know how to locate and use all of these sources before you can help your students do so. "Providing opportunities" for your students to use these sources requires you to develop appropriate assignments and to ensure students' accessibility to print, nonprint, and electronic reference sources in order to complete those assignments.

In achieving Competency 8.1, we recommend that you collaborate with a library media specialist if one is available in your school. School library media specialists have been specially trained to help you develop appropriate assignments and locate possible resources. They are also prepared to teach your students how to locate and use information from these resources.

You can minimally fulfill the intent of Competency 8.1 with a traditional research report assignment. For example, in social studies you could ask students to write research reports on individual states by using books, pamphlets, maps, and the Internet. Your goal would be to ensure that your students possess basic library research skills and know how to use the Internet.

In keeping with the learner-based inquiry emphasis of information literacy, however, you can encourage your students to develop their own research projects. These research projects can be traditional kinds of research projects, such as "Native American tribes" or "simple machines." Or, you can ask your students to identify a theme or themes, which can become a thematic unit (see Chapter 3). With a thematic unit, you can not only provide opportunities for students to locate and use a variety of sources (Competency 8.1), but you can also promote the integration of language arts across the curriculum (Competency 5.6). And because one of the sources mentioned in Competency 8.1 is electronic, you can also fulfill Competency 5.7—using instructional and information technologies to support literacy learning.

We encourage you to have students work with partners or small groups to complete at least part of an inquiry project. Research has established several advantages of cooperative learning—small groups working together toward a group goal (Johnson, Johnson, & Holubec, 1994; Slavin, 1987). The advantages of cooperative learning include improved achievement, greater effort, increased ability to think critically, and improved attitude and self-esteem. Researchers have noted that group learning also offers learners opportunities to observe and take part in the multiple roles often required to solve real-world problems, and to recognize and adjust for their own and others' misconceptions and ineffective strategies (Brown, Collins, & Duguid, 1989).

Competency 8.1 (as well as the related competencies 5.6 and 5.7) offers wonderful opportunities for cooperative learning. Students can work together to brainstorm research topics or themes, to locate a variety of sources, to gather information from these sources, and to communicate their findings.

Summary

By identifying the need for students to locate and use a variety of sources, Competency 8.1 acknowledges the critical role of information literacy in the Information Age. The competency, however, does not ask teachers to *teach* the skills and strategies involved in information literacy; rather, it asks teachers simply to provide students with opportunities to practice locating and using information from various sources. We suspect that teachers also need to teach students *how* to access, evaluate, organize, and use information from a variety of sources in order to become information literate. We hope that progress will be made on the recommendation of the American Library Association Presidential Committee on Information Literacy: "Teacher education and performance expectations should be modified to include information literacy concerns."

R E F E R E N C E S

*Recommended for teachers

_____. (March, 1998). A progress report on information literacy: An update on the American Library Association Presidential Committee on Information Literacy: Final Report [Online]. Available: http://www.infolit.org/documents/progress.html

American Association of School Librarians and the Association for Educational Communications and Technology. (1996). *Information standards for student learning*. Washington, DC: Author.

American Library Association Presidential Committee on Information Literacy. (1989). *Final Report*. Washington, DC: Author.

Bellingham Public Schools. (1996). Course outline: Information literacy and the net. Washington State University Web Site [On-line]. Available: http://www.bham.wednet.edu

Breivik, P. S. & Ford, B. J. (1993). Promoting learning in libraries through information literacy. *American Libraries, 24*(1), 98, 101–102.

Brown, J. S., Collins, A., & Duguid, P. (1989). Situated cognition and the culture of learning. *Educational Researcher, 18*(1), 32–42.

Carr, J. A. (1999). *Information literacy and teacher education*. ERIC Digest Number 97-4 [On-line]. Available: http://www.ericsp.org

Colorado Educational Media Association. (September, 1994). *Information literacy guidelines*. Colorado State Department of Education: State Library and Adult Education Office, Denver, CO. (ED 381163).

*Eisenberg, M., & Berkowitz, B. (1990). *Information problem-solving: The Big Six Skills Approach to library and information skills instruction*. Norwood, NJ: Ablex.

Humes, B. (September, 1999). *Understanding information literacy*. Office of Educational Research and National Institute on Postsecondary Education, Libraries, and Lifelong Learning [On-line]. Available: http://www.ed.gov/pubs/UnderLit/

Johnson, R. T., Johnson, D. W., & Holubec, E. J. (1987). Structuring cooperative learning: Lesson plans for teachers*. Edina, MN: Interaction Book Company.

*Slavin, R. E. (1987). *Cooperative learning: Student teams*. 2nd ed. Washington, DC: National Education Association.

17 Adjusting Reading Rate

COMPETENCY 8.2
Teach students to vary reading rate according to the purpose(s) and difficulty of the material.

Interpretation

Competency 8.2 recommends teaching a strategy used by proficient readers—varying reading rate according to the purpose(s) and difficulty of the material. For example, proficient readers will often read a novel for the purpose of enjoyment more rapidly than they will read a textbook for the purpose of studying for a test. Proficient readers will read difficult material more slowly, and they may reread sections that are especially challenging.

Related Research

The varying of reading rate is often classified as a metacognitive strategy. Metacognitive strategies involve planning, monitoring performance, and correcting errors when appropriate. Metacognition develops gradually, and is dependent on knowledge and experience (Bransford, Brown, & Cocking, 1999). Metacognitive development includes more detailed knowledge about what strategies are available, how they function, when they should be applied, and why they help comprehension. Research has shown that older and more proficient readers are more aware of problems that arise during reading and are more able to solve these problems (Dole, Duffy, Roehler, & Pearson, 1991; Garner, 1987; Paris, Wasik, & Turner, 1991).

Some research has focused specifically on the metacognitive strategy of varying reading according to purpose. Studies involving students of different age and ability levels have shown that the ability to adjust reading in response to purpose, similar to other metacognitive strategies, increases with age and ability level (see, for example, Brown, Armbruster, & Baker, 1986). For example, skimming is one activity that reflects students' understanding of adjusting reading rate for purpose. In one study (Kobasigawa, Ransom, & Holland, 1980) fourth, sixth, and eighth graders were asked to find specific types of information in short passages and were then interviewed to determine their awareness of skimming techniques. Children at all levels were able to skim when explicitly instructed how to do so, but spontaneous skimming as a strategy to meet task requirements developed only gradually with age. Even at the college level, some students read everything at the same rate, regardless of its difficulty or their reasons for reading (Bond & Tinker, 1973).

Research has also shown that instruction in particular metacognitive strategies can be extremely helpful in facilitating comprehension. While we are unaware of research focusing on teaching students how to vary reading rate according to purpose or difficulty of material, we think it is reasonable to assume that such instruction would be as helpful as other instruction in metacognitive strategies.

What Does This Mean for You, the Teacher?

You should teach the strategy of varying reading rate the same way you teach other comprehension strategies: by using direct instruction, as discussed in Chapter 11. First, you should identify, explain, and model the strategy. Model varying reading rate by "thinking aloud" how you vary your reading rate when reading for different purposes and with different types of materials. For example, you can model reading a single text for purposes as varied as reading for enjoyment, reading to identify an appropriate title, reading to answer a specific question, and reading to study for an unspecified test. Also, you can model reading for varied purposes with texts of different genres, such as a poem, a newspaper article, or a biography.

After you identify, explain, and model how to vary reading rate, you can provide guided practice (with scaffolding) as your students practice reading different types of materials for different purposes. Next, have your students use the strategy independently as you monitor their ability to vary their reading rate according to the purpose(s) and difficulty of the material.

The fact that this competency is placed in the section on study strategies might lead you to believe that the strategy is more appropriate to teach during the later elementary years. You can, however, begin to teach the strategy of varying reading rate with students in the primary grades. For example, if you are a primary grade teacher, you can point out to your students that they naturally vary the rate of their oral reading according to their familiarity with the material. That is, they read familiar (easier) material more rapidly than unfamiliar (more difficult) material. You can also begin to teach reading for different purposes. For example, you could teach skimming by directing your students to look through a story quickly to find all words that contain the phonogram "at" or to find all the color names.

Summary

Competency 8.2 advocates teaching the metacognitive strategy of varying reading rate according to purpose and difficulty of reading material. Research has shown that, as with other metacognitive strategies, older and more proficient readers are more aware of how and when to adjust reading rate than are younger and less proficient readers. Teachers should teach this strategy as they would other comprehension strategies—using direct instruction and beginning early.

REFERENCES

Bond, G. L., & Tinker, M. A. (1973). *Reading difficulties: Their diagnosis and correction.* 3rd ed. New York: Appleton-Century-Crofts.

Bransford, J. D., Brown, A. L., & Cocking, R. R. (Eds.). (1999). *How people learn: Brain, mind, experience, and school.* Washington, DC: National Academy Press.

Brown, A. L., Armbruster, B. B., & Baker, L. (1986). The role of metacognition in reading and studying. In J. Orasanu (Ed.), *Reading comprehension: From research to practice* (pp. 49–75). Hillsdale, NJ: Erlbaum.

Dole, J. A., Duffy, G. G., Roehler, L. R., & Pearson, P. D. (1991). Moving from the old to the new: Research on reading comprehension instruction. *Review of Educational Research, 61*(2), 239–264.

Garner, R. (1987). *Metacognition and reading comprehension.* Norwood, NJ: Ablex.

Kobasigawa, A., Ransom, C. C., & Holland, C. J. (1980). Children's knowledge about skimming. *Alberta Journal of Educational Research, 26,* 169–182.

Paris, S. G., Wasik, B. A., & Turner, J. C. (1991). The development of strategic readers. In R. Barr, M. L. Kamil, P. Mosenthal, & P. D. Pearson (Eds.), *Handbook of Reading Research,* Vol. II (pp. 609–640). New York: Longman.

18 Time-Management Strategies

COMPETENCY 8.3
Teach students effective time-management strategies.

Interpretation

Competency 8.3 recommends teaching students how to manage their time as one specific study strategy. Time management is certainly an essential skill, not only during the school years, but also during the rest of life. In school, students' time is managed mostly by the school schedule; however, students have to manage their own time at home and learn how to allocate enough time to get their work done.

We are puzzled by the inclusion of teaching time-management strategies in competencies for reading professionals, however. Time management is a broader instructional goal that applies to all academic areas. We know of no particular time-management strategies that are specific to reading or writing.

Related Research

Time management as a study strategy for elementary, middle school, and secondary students has not been a popular topic for researchers over the past two decades. We were able to locate only one relatively recent research study. Delucchi, Rohwer, and Thomas (1987) investigated the amount of time junior high, senior high, and college students spent studying outside of class. They found no correlation between self-reported total study time and two measures of academic achievement—final test score and grade in course. The researchers concluded that academic success depended not on total time spent studying, but on how the students used this time. In other words, effective time management appeared to be a key to the academic success of the students in this study. Therefore, at least one study suggests the potential value of teaching time-management strategies. We could locate no research, however, that suggests what effective time-management strategies are or how they should be taught.

What Does This Mean for You, the Teacher?

A large number of handbooks or manuals on study strategies exist, particularly for secondary and postsecondary students. Despite the lack of research on time management as a study strategy, many of these publications contain sections on time management, and a few focus exclusively on time management. We have selected what appears to us to be some sound advice from handbooks published during this decade (e.g., Gall, Gall, Jacobsen, & Bullock, 1990; Irvin & Rose, 1995; Lewis, 1992):

1. Teach students to assess their use of time. Your students should be aware of how they spend their time at school, in extracurricular activities, watching television, socializing and talking on the phone, doing homework, sleeping, and so forth. Students should know how much time they spend studying and how and where they might be wasting time.

2. Teach students to use an assignment notebook. You should encourage your students to record each assignment and the date it is due. When the assignment has been completed, the student can check it off. Both you and the student's parents can monitor the assignment notebook to determine whether assignments have been recorded and completed.

3. Help students set priorities. Your students need to learn that some activities are essential and others are less important, not only for activities outside of school, but also for assignments in school. Help your students understand that some assignments are worth more (in terms of grades) or require more time to complete than other assignments.

4. Teach students to schedule their time. You can help your students develop monthly, weekly, and daily schedules for study time needed to complete assignments. Students can use their monthly and weekly schedules to plan what they must do each day to ensure that all work is done on time. Help your students keep in mind the relative priorities of assignments in planning their schedules. Periodically work with your students to review, evaluate, and revise their schedules.

5. Teach students to break large assignments into manageable parts. For large, long-term assignments like writing a research paper, you can help students break the task down into smaller subtasks, such as locating resources, taking notes, making an outline, writing a draft, revising based on feedback, and writing the final paper. Then, working back from the due date, help your students set a schedule for completing each subtask. As work on the research paper progresses, ask your students if they are keeping to their schedules and help them revise their schedules as needed.

6. Help students become more efficient. Encourage students to get organized, for example, by keeping an assignment notebook, by planning a reasonable schedule, and by having the proper materials on hand. Provide suggestions for how students can use spare time more effectively, for example, by reviewing spelling words while waiting for the bus, by taking full advantage of study hall time, and by reducing the time spent watching TV or talking on the phone.

7. Encourage parent involvement. You can send letters or newsletters to parents, encouraging them to help their children develop time-management skills. For example, you can suggest that parents establish and monitor a scheduled time for homework, monitor the assignment notebook, and reward their children for completing assignments on time. You can also suggest that parents discuss their own time-management strategies, such as sharing their personal calendars.

Summary

Although we do not consider time management to be a critical instructional goal for reading professionals, we have offered a few suggestions for helping students manage their time. These suggestions, however, were gleaned from study manuals and handbooks rather than derived from research.

REFERENCES

*Recommended for teachers

Delucchi, J. J., Rohwer, W. D., & Thomas, J. W. (1987). Study time allocation as a function of grade level and course characteristics. *Contemporary Educational Psychology, 12*(4), 365–380.

*Gall, M. D., Gall, J. P., Jacobsen, D. R., & Bullock, T. L. (1990). *Tools for learning: A guide to teaching study skills*. Alexandria, VA: Association for Supervision and Curriculum Development.

Irvin, J. L., & Rose, E. O. (1995). *Starting early with study skills: A week-by-week guide for elementary students*. Boston: Allyn & Bacon.

Lewis, N. J. (1992). *Student time manager*. Oakville, ON, Canada: Trilobyte Press.

CHAPTER

19 Organizing and Remembering Information

COMPETENCY 8.4
Teach students strategies to organize and remember information.

Interpretation

This competency implies that reading professionals should teach students two specific kinds of strategies: strategies for organizing information and strategies for remembering information. Organizing information can help students both comprehend and remember information. In fact, *all* study strategies are intended to help students comprehend and remember information. Therefore, we believe the intent of this competency is: Teach students strategies for organizing information *in order to* comprehend and remember it.

Related Research

Most research on organizing information in the last two decades has involved the role of text organization. Research has established a strong relationship between the organization of text and reading comprehension: (1) better organized text is better comprehended; (2) the more students are aware of and strategically use text organization, the better their comprehension; (3) explicit instruction in text organization facilitates comprehension (Dickson, Simmons, & Kameenui, 1995). Only the third finding is directly relevant here.

Research supports the effectiveness of two types of instruction related to text organization: instruction in the physical presentation of text and instruction about text structure (Dickson, Simmons, & Kameenui, 1995). Instruction about the physical presentation of text is about text features such as headings and subheadings, location of main ideas, an author's direct statements of importance, and "signal words" emphasizing text structures, such as *first, in contrast, as a result*. Instruction in text structure refers to the top-level organizational patterns that show how the text ideas are logically connected. Two types of text structures have been investigated: the structure of narratives or stories, and the structures of expository, or informational, text.

Many studies have been designed to investigate the benefits of teaching students about the structure of stories. These studies usually involve instruction in a simplified version of story grammars, which are representations of the general structure of conventional stories. Typically, the simplified story grammar categories taught to children are *setting, problem, goal, actions*, and *outcome*. In a number of studies, comprehension and memory for stories improved following instruction in story structure (Dickson, Simmons, & Kameenui, 1995; Pearson & Fielding, 1991).

One form of instruction about expository text structure uses the physical presentation of text—headings, subheadings, and paragraphs—to construct summaries (see the discussion of hierarchical summarization strategy in Chapter 11). Another form of instruction has focused on expository text structures. Whereas most conventional stories have a single underlying structure, expository text comes in several different structures. The identity and names of these structures vary somewhat from researcher to researcher, but a typical list includes *enumeration, sequence* or *time order, comparison–contrast, cause–effect*, and *problem–solution*. In several research studies, students were taught expository text structures by making visual representations of the structures. In some cases, these visual representations were used as the basis for note taking or summarizing text. These visual representations vary in both form and name (e.g., networking, flowcharting, Con Struct, mapping, conceptual frames, conceptual mapping, graphic organizers). Whatever the form or name, instruction in some type of visual representation of text has consistently shown benefits in comprehension for students of differing abilities (Dickson, Simmons, & Kameenui, 1995; National Reading Panel, 2000). Indeed, the research supporting instruction in expository text structure is so strong that Pearson and Fielding (1991) claimed to have found "incredibly positive support for just about any approach to text structure instruction for expository text" (p. 832).

What Does This Mean for You, the Teacher?

Research strongly supports teaching your students text structures and how to use them as tools for comprehending and remembering information. According to research, such instruction can be especially helpful for less able and ESL students. Because expository text is more difficult for students than narrative text (Dickson, Simmons, & Kameenui, 1995), you should be especially diligent about teaching expository text structures.

Your instruction should have three basic parts. First, explain the importance of using text structure as a way for your students to organize their learning; second, help them identify text structures; third, give them a strategy, such as constructing graphic organizers, to help them organize content, monitor comprehension, and meet task demands such as answering questions or writing reports.

One way to teach expository text structures is to help students identify the ways authors denote a particular text structure through the use of headings and subheadings, topic sentences, or signal words such as *first, in contrast, as a result*. (See Armbruster, Anderson, & Ostertag [1989]; McGee & Richgels [1985]; or Piccolo [1987] for examples of expository text structures and how they are signaled in text.)

You can also reinforce the concept of text structures by teaching students to use different kinds of graphic organizers to identify the important information high-lighted within a particular text structure. For example, to teach a comparison–contrast structure, you can use a Venn diagram in which students draw two intersecting circles and label each circle with one of the concepts being compared. Then students write similarities in the overlapping portion of the circles and differ-ences within the appropriate circle outside the common area. An alternative for teaching the comparison–contrast structure is a table or matrix that has the concepts to be compared and the features on which they are being compared as the row and column headings. To teach the time-order text structure, you can use a time line (for historical events) or a simple flow chart (for directions or procedures). (See Hyerle [1996]; Jones, Pierce, & Hunter [1988/89], or Parks & Black [1992] for many ex-amples of graphic organizers.) Because expository text is difficult for many readers, you will probably want to begin with short, easy texts to demonstrate the strategy of constructing graphic organizers.

In addition to text structure-based graphic organizers, you can teach students to develop other forms of graphic organizers. The simplest form is probably webbing, a form of graphic outlining in which students depict subtopics and details around their main topic. As another example, semantic mapping uses a graphic organizer for learn-ing sets of conceptually related words (e.g., Heimlich & Pittelman, 1986). In develop-ing a semantic map, students identify relationships among words, explain how the words are related, and place them in conceptual categories.

Besides teaching text structure, you can help students learn to organize infor-mation using other strategies (although, surprisingly, many of these other strategies have not yet been thoroughly researched). For example, you may teach students to outline text content. You may, of course, teach a formal outline structure, but that is difficult for students to learn. Or, you may teach them to outline information infor-mally by simply listing topics and then indenting or using bullets or dashes for less important information.

Another way to help students organize and remember information is to have them learn to take notes. Standard suggestions for note taking include: (1) use short phrases rather than complete sentences; (2) use your own words; (3) record only the most important ideas; (4) don't be concerned about spelling, punctuation, or hand-writing; (5) use abbreviations, initials, or other devices to speed the process. These suggestions can be difficult for students to follow; most students will need plenty of direct instruction to become proficient note takers.

Some variations on note taking may be easier for students to learn. One possi-bility is two-column notes. Students use one column to record information from the text, and the other to reflect on that information in a way that encourages them to connect the new information to their prior knowledge. You can have your students label the headings for the columns in a variety of ways, for example, direct quote/personal response, facts/questions, or new concepts/familiar concepts (see Harvey, 1998, for additional examples). You can encourage students to keep a journal in which they record their notes in a two-column format.

Summary

In summary, research has shown a strong relationship between students' ability to identify and use text organization and their comprehension and memory for text. Furthermore, explicit instruction in text structure has been very successful in improving comprehension. Therefore, we strongly recommend that you teach text structures, especially text structures for the more difficult expository text, as a way to help students learn to organize information. We discussed some other ways to help students organize information, such as outlining and note taking, which we believe to be helpful as well; however, strong research support for these strategies is not currently available.

REFERENCES

*Recommended for teachers

*Armbruster, B. B., Anderson, T. H., & Ostertag, J. (1989). Teaching text structure to improve reading and writing. *The Reading Teacher, 43*(2), 130–137.

Dickson, S. V., Simmons, D. C., & Kameenui, E. J. (1995). *Text organization and its relation to reading comprehension: A synthesis of the research* (Tech. Rep. No. 17). Eugene, OR: University of Oregon, National Center to Improve the Tools of Educators.

*Harvey, S. (1998). *Nonfiction matters: Reading, writing, and research in grades 3–8*. York, ME: Stenhouse.

*Heimlich, J. E., & Pittelman, S. O. (1986). *Semantic mapping: Classroom applications*. Newark, DE: International Reading Association.

*Hyerle, D. (1996). *Visual tools for constructing knowledge*. Alexandria, VA: Association for Supervision and Curriculum Development.

*Jones, B. F., Pierce, J., & Hunter, B. (1988/89). Teaching students to construct graphic representations. *Educational Leadership, 46*(4), 20–25.

*McGee, L. M., & Richgels, D. J. (1985). Teaching expository text structure to elementary students. *The Reading Teacher, 38*, 739–748.

National Reading Panel. (2000). *Teaching children to read: An evidence-based assessment of the scientific research literature on reading and its implications for reading instruction*. Washington, DC: National Institute of Child Health and Human Development.

*Parks, S., & Black, H. (1992). *Organizing thinking, Book I*. Pacific Grove, CA: Critical Thinking Press & Software.

Pearson, P., & Fielding, L. (1991). Comprehension instruction. In R. Barr, M. L. Kamil, P. Mosenthal, & P. D. Pearson (Eds.), *Handbook of reading research*, Vol. 2 (pp. 815–860). White Plains, NY: Longman.

*Piccolo, J. (1987). Expository text structure: Teaching and learning strategies. *The Reading Teacher, 40*, 838–847.

20 Test-Taking Strategies

COMPETENCY 8.5
Teach test-taking strategies.

Interpretation

This competency is quite clear. Test-taking strategies include following directions, pacing oneself appropriately during timed tests, reasoning deductively, guessing strategically, checking answers, becoming familiar with test formats, and using answer sheets correctly. The goal of teaching such strategies is to improve test scores, particularly on standardized tests.

Related Research

Since the 1980s there has been increasing emphasis on student test scores as indicators of educational effectiveness. Many states have mandated achievement testing to determine the quality of education in the state, but the scores have also been used to reflect the effectiveness of school districts, schools, teachers, and students. Because of the significant contingencies associated with achievement test scores, Popham (1991) refers to such legislatively mandated tests as "high stakes tests." A result of high-stakes testing is that administrators and teachers are increasingly under pressure to raise the test scores of their students.

Among the many ways to raise test scores, some are appropriate while others (e.g., cheating) are clearly not (Mehrens & Kaminski, 1989; Popham, 1991). One appropriate way to enhance test performance is to teach general strategies for taking tests, such as those listed above. It is important that test results reflect the students' mastery of the content tested rather than their test-taking abilities, but students vary in their familiarity with and ability to take tests of various kinds. Promoters of instruction in test-taking strategies claim that students will obtain higher and more valid test scores when deficiencies in test-taking strategies are eliminated.

Popham (1991), though, cautions that instruction in test-taking strategies is only appropriate if it is "not excessively lengthy" (p. 14) so that it distracts from the student's ongoing education. According to Popham, appropriate preparation for tests should raise not only test scores, but also mastery of the content being tested. In other words, as Matter (1986) put it: "Ideally, test preparation activities should not be additional activities imposed upon teachers. Rather, they should be incorporated into the regular, ongoing instructional activities whenever possible" (p. 10).

Unfortunately, there is currently inconclusive research support for the claim that teaching test-taking strategies increases students' performance on achievement tests. In a review of the effectiveness of training programs in test-taking skills on elementary and secondary achievement, Samson (1985) concluded that only training extending over a period of five weeks or more can result in significant improvements in students' scores on achievement tests. Such lengthy instruction, of course, violates Popham's advocacy of fairly brief preparation for tests that does not seriously distract from ongoing classroom instruction.

In a more rigorous meta-analysis of research involving elementary students only, Scruggs, White, and Bennion (1986) concluded that "training children in test-taking skills has limited effects on achievement scores" (p. 79). Like Samson (1985), Scruggs and his colleagues concluded that longer training programs (exceeding four weeks) were generally more effective than shorter training programs. Specifically, for children in grades four to six a shorter amount of training may be effective, but for children in grades one to three more training is necessary. Their results also suggested that training in test-taking skills may be differentially effective for various subgroups of children. For example, such training may be more effective for lower SES children than higher SES children, though the researchers cautioned that this result should be treated very tentatively pending further research. Finally, in their analysis of instructional studies in test-taking strategies, Scruggs, White, and Bennion were unable to find more specific information about what types of training are most effective, primarily because the researchers of the studies they reviewed failed to describe their instructional programs in sufficient detail.

In summary, research suggests that even extensive instruction (more than four to five weeks) in test-taking strategies provided by trained researchers and educators has only limited effectiveness. Furthermore, research fails to reveal more specific information about the relative effectiveness of various strategies or how they might best be taught.

What Does This Mean for You, the Teacher?

In light of the research on test-taking strategies, we have little to offer in the way of recommendations regarding Competency 8.5. A critical question is whether teachers should spend time teaching test-taking strategies rather than spending the same amount of time teaching reading and writing. We agree with Scruggs, White, and Bennion that "The answer is not clear cut" (p. 79) at the present time. Our opinion, however, is that most of the instuctional time of reading professionals would be better spent teaching reading and writing strategies than test-taking strategies.

Even if you wished to teach test-taking strategies, research does not suggest which specific strategies you should teach or how you should teach them. However, it may well be helpful for you to teach your students strategies such as following directions, responding to particular test formats, and using time wisely during tests. It will be particularly beneficial to the extent that you can incorporate insruction in such test-taking strategies into your regular classroom instruction, perhaps, within the context of your normal classroom tests.

Summary

We urge caution regarding Competency 8.5: Teach test-taking strategies. Research does not provide strong support for this recommendation; nor does research suggest what test-taking strategies to teach or how to teach them. Limited instruction about some test-taking strategies *may* be helpful if it does not detract from instruction in reading and writing.

R E F E R E N C E S

Matter, M. K. (1986). Legitimate ways to prepare students for testing: Being up front to protect your behind. In J. Hall, & P. Wolmut (Eds.), *National association of test directors 1986 symposia* (pp. 10–11). Oklahoma City, OK: Oklahoma City Public Schools.

Mehrens, W. A., & Kaminski, J. (1989). Methods for improving standardized test scores: Fruitful, fruitless, or fraudulent? *Educational Measurement: Issues and Practice, 8*(1), 14–22.

Popham, W. J. (1991). Appropriateness of teachers' test-preparation practices. *Educational Measurement: Issues and Practice, 10*, 12–15.

Samson, G. E. (1985). Effect of training in test-taking skills on achievement test performance: A quantitative synthesis. *Journal of Educational Research, 78*(5), 261–266.

Scruggs, T. E., White, K. R., & Bennion, K. (1986). Teaching test-taking skills to elementary-grade students: A meta-analysis. *The Elementary School Journal, 87*(1), 69–82.

21 Writing Process

COMPETENCY 9.1
Teach students planning strategies most appropriate for particular kinds of writing.

COMPETENCY 9.2
Teach students to draft, revise, and edit their writing.

Interpretation

We include Competencies 9.1 and 9.2 in one chapter because, together, they describe the process approach to teaching writing. This approach refers to five stages of the writing process: prewriting (or planning), drafting (or composing), revising, editing, and publishing. Together, the two IRA competencies advocate teaching four of these five writing stages. The fact that Competency 9.1 focuses on the prewriting or planning stage only while Competency 9.2 encompasses the three stages of drafting, revising, and editing appears to reflect the IRA's relatively greater emphasis on the first stage of the writing process.

Related Research

Before turning to research on the writing process, we comment on the appropriateness of including writing in the IRA *Standards for Reading Professionals*. Reading and writing share similar underlying cognitive processes. Research shows that writing improves reading achievement, reading results in better writing performance, and combined reading–writing instruction leads to improvements in both areas (Tierney & Shanahan, 1991). Furthermore, engaging students in combined reading and writing experiences promotes a higher level of thinking than instruction in either process alone (Braunger & Lewis, 1997). Therefore, it is appropriate that the IRA competencies include writing.

Beginning in the 1970s, researchers became interested in the cognitive processes of writers, including students, as they wrote or composed. In the early 1980s, some researchers (e.g., de Beaugrande, 1984; Bracewell, Frederiksen, & Frederiksen, 1982; Flower & Hayes, 1981) began to develop models of the composing process of expert writers. According to these models, writing is a complex goal-directed, problem-solving process that consists of a number of subprocesses. These subprocesses include planning (writers set goals, generate ideas, and organize information), translating or transcribing text (writers transform ideas into written form), and reviewing (writers evaluate, edit, and revise the text). Rather than a simple linear process, writing is viewed as a recursive process, in which writers constantly recycle through the subprocesses. The writing process is influenced by the writer's prior knowledge and his or her goal in writing.

While cognitive psychologists developed models of the composing process of expert writers, the process approach to teaching writing in elementary schools was influenced much more by Donald Graves's (1983) book, *Writing: Teachers and Children at Work*. Graves popularized a five-stage model consisting of prewriting (or planning), drafting (or composing), revising, editing, and publishing. Today this model is known as the writing process (or process writing). In *prewriting*, writers select a topic, consider content, and decide what form their writing will take. In *drafting*, writers get their words down on paper, wrestling with issues such as idea development and elaboration and choice of language. *Revising* is an ongoing process of refining and redrafting the piece. *Editing*, the final stage of revision, includes changes in content (wording and idea elaboration) as well as attention to mechanics (spelling and punctuation). In *publishing*, writers publicly share the final copy of their writing. As with the models developed by cognitive psychologists, the Graves's model is also recursive rather than linear, with writers continuously cycling through the stages.

For almost two decades, many teachers have embraced the process approach to teaching writing. Process approaches in classrooms, however, have not been universally successful (Dyson & Freedman, 1991). The lack of success may be partly due to confusion over exactly what the process approach is. In many cases, the intended recursive process has been transformed into a mechanized procedure consisting of an invariable sequence of steps: brainstorm, draft, conference, revise, publish (Dyson & Freedman, 1991; Newkirk & Atwell, 1988).

What Does This Mean for You, the Teacher?

Although research does not yet provide strong support for the process approach to teaching writing, it seems to us to be the most coherent approach to writing instruction currently available. It is important to keep in mind that writing is a recursive process that varies from individual to individual. It should not become a rigid, linear procedure.

The process approach to writing is probably most often implemented in classrooms in the form of the *writing workshop*, which is based on the ideas behind writing as a process (Atwell, 1987; Calkins, 1991, 1994; Graves, 1994). Writing workshop is a period of classroom time set aside for students to be immersed in the writing process. A common framework for a writing workshop is: (1) a "minilesson," (2) a period of sustained writing with conferences, and (3) a time for sharing writing. A minilesson is a short instructional segment (typically no longer than ten minutes) in which you teach a particular topic or skill that several of your students need in order to progress with their writing. For example, you might teach a minilesson on quotation marks as students demonstrate a need to use quotation marks in their writing.

You should spend the majority of the writing workshop time with the children engaged in actual writing, both individually and in collaboration with peers. During this time, your students will be working recursively through the first four stages of the writing process. During the prewriting stage, they will select a topic, consider content (perhaps through brainstorming), decide a form for their writing, and anticipate the writing to follow. During drafting, your students will start getting their words on paper as they develop and elaborate ideas and work on language precision. While drafting, they will continue to anticipate the content and design of their work. Revising will probably be difficult to separate from drafting, because many writers revise their content, form, and language as they draft. Editing is the final revision stage in which your students will attend to wording and idea elaboration as well as mechanics (spelling and punctuation).

As students are working through the writing process, you can circulate, observe their activity and progress, identify their needs, and hold conferences with them to provide assistance. You may also want to include peer conferences, in which small groups of children share their in-progress writing with one another and receive assistance from their peers.

Finally, you can end the session with open sharing, in which your students, one at a time, sit in the Author's Chair, share their writing with the whole group, and receive feedback. A more formal way of sharing is through publishing, in which children "publish" final drafts of polished written pieces, often in the form of books to be displayed in the classroom or shared with others.

Key principles of the writing workshop are the need for students to have regular periods of extended time for writing, to choose their own topics, to receive helpful feedback and response, to learn mechanics in context, to know adults who write, and to read widely (Atwell, 1987). In addition, you will want to see that your students write for a variety of real purposes and audiences and that they learn to take control and responsibility for their own writing. (See Atwell, 1987; Calkins, 1986, 1991; and Graves, 1983, 1994, for detailed practical advice on how to teach process writing.)

Summary

Despite the lack of research support for the effectiveness of the process approach to teaching writing, we support the IRA's advocacy of teaching the writing process. We are puzzled, however, as to why the IRA (1) never identified the stages listed in Competency 9.1 and 9.2 as "the writing process," and (2) chose to separate the writing process into two separate competencies. By separating planning (prewriting) from drafting, revising, and editing, the IRA is implicitly transforming what should be conceived of as a smooth, iterative process into a sequence of procedures. In addition, placing planning (prewriting) in one competency and drafting, revising, and editing in another competency delivers a message about the relative importance of the stages of the writing process, with the implication that planning is of greater importance than drafting, revising, and editing. We agree that planning is very important in instruction, especially because prior research on the writing process has shown that children do relatively little planning (Flower & Hayes, 1981). We do not, however, think that it is any more important than drafting, revising, or editing. Our preference would be to combine IRA Competencies 9.1 and 9.2 into a single competency: Teach the writing process (or, the process approach to writing).

REFERENCES

*Recommended for teachers

*Atwell, N. (1987). *In the middle: Writing, reading, and learning with adolescents.* Portsmouth, NH: Heinemann.

de Beaugrande, R. (1982). Psychology and composition: Past, present, and future. In M. Nystrand (Ed.), *What writers know: The language, process and structure of written discourse* (pp. 211–168). New York: Academic Press.

Bracewell, R. J., Frederiksen, C. H., & Frederiksen, J. D. (1982). Cognitive processes in composing and comprehending discourse. *Educational Psychologist, 17,* 146–164.

Braunger, J., & Lewis, J. P. (1997). *Building a knowledge base in reading.* Portland, OR: Northwest Regional Educational Laboratory.

*Calkins, L. M. (1991). *Living between the lines.* Portsmouth, NH: Heinemann.

*Calkins, L. M. (1994). *The art of teaching writing.* Portsmouth, NH: Heinemann.

Dyson, A. H., & Freedman, S. W. (1991). Writing. In J. Flood, J. M. Jensen, D. Lapp, & J. R. Squire (Eds.), *Handbook of research on teaching the English language arts* (pp. 754–774). New York: Macmillan.

Flower, L., & Hayes, J. R. (1981). A cognitive process theory of writing. *College Composition and Communication 32,* 365–387.

*Graves, D. H. (1983). Writing: Teachers and children at work. Portsmouth, NH: Heinemann.

*Graves, D. H. (1994). *A fresh look at writing.* Portsmouth, NH: Heinemann.

*Newkirk, T., & Atwell, N. (Eds.). (1988). *Understanding writing.* 2nd ed. Portsmouth, NH: Heinemann.

Tierney, R. J., & Shanahan, T. (1991). Research on the reading–writing relationship: Interactions, transactions, and outcomes. In R. Barr, M. L. Kamil, P. Mosenthal, & P. D. Pearson (Eds.), *Handbook of reading research,* Vol. 2 (pp. 246–280). New York: Longman.

22 Conventions of Written English

COMPETENCY 9.3
Teach students the conventions of standard written English needed to edit their compositions.

Interpretation

Another competency, Competency 7.5, encourages teachers to teach conventions of standard written English to improve reading comprehension. Competency 9.3 again encourages teachers to teach conventions of standard written English, but this time so that students are able to edit their compositions and, presumably, improve the quality of their writing. As with Competency 7.5, we will use the definition of conventions of written English provided in the IRA/NCTE publication, *Standards for the English Language Arts* (1996): Conventions of written English include grammar, punctuation, and spelling. An elaboration of the edit stage of process writing referred to in Competency 9.2 (see Chapter 21), Competency 9.3 specifies that students should be focusing on grammar, punctuation, and spelling as they edit.

Related Research

Grammar and Punctuation

Schools have provided formal instruction in grammar since the last half of the eighteenth century. Traditional school grammar instruction includes teaching the definitions and appropriate uses of parts of speech, the structures and function of various types of phrases, clauses, and sentences, and certain rules of usage, such as "Never end a sentence with a preposition" or "Never use 'ain't." Traditional grammar instruction is primarily characterized by memorizing definitions, practice in identifying the elements of sentences, analyzing sentences into their constituent structures (parsing), and informing students about common usage errors and the mechanics of writing, including punctuation. The assumption underlying traditional grammar instruction is that grammar study will improve students' use of language, particularly their writing (Straw, 1994).

Tradition, however, is not supported by research. Research across nine decades has overwhelmingly shown that teaching traditional school grammar does not have a beneficial effect on students' writing, including their use of "correct" conventions (Hillocks & Smith, 1991). The following is an oft-quoted statement from a review of writing research by Braddock, Lloyd-Jones, and Schoer (1963):

> The conclusion can be stated in strong and unqualified terms: the teaching of grammar has a negligible, or, because it usually displaces some instruction and practice in actual composition, even a harmful effect on the improvement of writing (pp. 37–38).

Almost two decades later, another comprehensive review of writing research by Hillocks (1986) concludes

> The study of traditional school grammar (i.e., the definition of parts of speech, the parsing of sentences, etc.) has no effect on raising the quality of student writing. . . .Taught in certain ways, grammar and mechanics instruction has a deleterious effect on student writing. In some studies a heavy emphasis on mechanics and usage (e.g., marking every error) resulted in significant losses in overall quality. School boards, administrators, and teachers who impose the systematic study of traditional school grammar on their students over lengthy periods of time in the name of teaching writing do them a gross disservice which should not be tolerated by anyone concerned with the effective teaching of good writing (p. 248).

One possible explanation for the lack of effectiveness of grammar instruction is that grammar may not be related to the features of writing that are typically associated with quality. Writing is usually evaluated by content, organization, and style. Knowledge of grammar, however, does not help with content or organization; its greatest potential contribution is to style (Noguchi, 1991). Another reason instruction in grammar may not improve writing is related to how grammar is taught. Traditional grammar has been taught as a teacher-directed analytic activity with an emphasis on correctness. Students learn formal rules of grammar and practice skills in isolation. Current thinking, however, is that language use involves the synthesis and construction of meaning for authentic purposes of communication. Therefore, the traditional instruction in analysis may actually interfere with language's constructive processes (Straw, 1994).

Despite consistent research findings about the lack of effectiveness of teaching formal, traditional grammar, teachers, as well as other community members, are likely to reject this finding because of a deep concern that students' written products are "correct" in terms of written English conventions (Hillocks & Smith, 1991). Because many teachers themselves are convinced that they benefited at least somewhat from the formal study of grammar (Weaver, 1998), teachers still believe that "grammar provides the basis for 'correctness' in writing, for putting commas and periods in the conventional places" (Hillocks & Smith, 1991, p. 600). As Taylor (1986) puts it, "teachers working with student writing know that their students need some knowledge of language and its conventions" (p. 95). Therefore, popular opinion will continue to call for and expect grammar instruction in language arts instruction (Hartwell, 1994).

If traditional school grammar instruction is ineffective, how should students be taught grammar? Research conducted since the mid-1960s has investigated the effect of instruction in more functional approaches to grammar—that is, approaches that build on students' tacit knowledge of language and thus resemble more closely the synthetic nature of language use (Straw, 1994). For example, a large number of studies have investigated sentence combining and sentence construction. In sentence combining, students are asked to combine two or more given sentences into an appropriate single sentence. In sentence construction, students generate their own information prior to constructing sentences. Studies on sentence combining and construction have found significant effects on writing, particularly in syntactic control and facility (Hillocks, 1986; Straw, 1994).

In keeping with a functional approach, some research on grammar and writing suggests that the most effective way to teach grammar and English conventions is in the context of meaningful reading and writing (Hillocks, 1986; Noguchi, 1991; Weaver, 1996, 1998). We will have more to say about such instruction in the section, What Does This Mean for You, the Teacher?

Spelling

Chapter 9 describes some of the latest research related to learning to spell.

What Does This Mean for You, the Teacher?

Grammar and Punctuation.   Some research, as well as the advice of most advocates of the process approach to teaching writing (see Chapter 21), suggest that you should teach the conventions of written English functionally, in the context of its use. According to Atwell (1987), Calkins (1994), Graves (1994), and Weaver (1996, 1998), students can best learn to use conventions when they understand the role of conventions in conveying or clarifying meaning in the materials they read and write. These educators claim that grammar and written English conventions can be taught as part of the writing process, particularly during the editing and revising stages (see Chapter 21).

What aspects of grammar should you teach? Weaver (1996, 1998), who suggests "a minimum of grammar for maximum benefits," recommends five categories of grammatical concepts as the focus of instruction: (1) teaching concepts of subject, verb, sentence, clause, phrase, and related concepts for editing; (2) teaching style through sentence combining and sentence generating; (3) teaching sentence sense and style through the manipulation of syntactic elements; (4) teaching the power of dialects and dialects of power; and (5) teaching punctuation and mechanics for convention, clarity, and style (1996, pp. 142–144; 1998, pp. 21–23). Weaver describes each of these categories in greater detail in the cited sources.

When should you teach these aspects of grammar? Again, according to Weaver (1996, 1998), the appropriate timing of grammar instruction varies from individual to individual. She recommends that teachers examine the aspects of grammar mentioned in the previous paragraph and their own students' writing, and then offer appropriate guidance when needed. Weaver acknowledges that some basic grammatical concepts may need to be taught in addition to or aside from the writing process. She states,

> At the very least, I would recommend that teachers in a school or school system decide what their own students should be taught at each level, with considerable overlap. Better yet, teachers could collectively decide what the teachers at each grade level should be responsible for teaching, but only to the students who demonstrate the need or readiness for these predetermined concepts and skills in their writing (1998, p. 24).

How can you teach the conventions of written English? One way to teach conventions is to show students how authors use conventions in the materials your class is reading. For example, in beginning reading materials, you can point out the way punctuation marks are used. For somewhat older students, you can focus on identifying and working with parts of speech as they appear in reading materials. In materials for more advanced readers, you can call attention to the author's use of various kinds of sentence structures in order to create interest and variety. Another obvious place to teach the conventions of written English is during the writing process (see also Chapter 21). First, you can teach skills in minilessons, either to the whole class when almost everyone needs the skill, or to a small group when only some students need help with the skill. Second, you can provide instruction during teacher conferences, as you move from a focus on content to a focus on editing. Third, you can encourage your students to work together in groups to edit each other's writing or to edit their own work. You may find it helpful to teach your students proofreading marks for editing. You may also want to provide a checklist of conventions your students should look for when editing their peers' or their own work.

Spelling

Suggestions for teaching spelling are given in Chapter 9.

Summary

Competency 9.3 urges teachers to teach the conventions of written English—grammar, punctuation, and spelling—needed to edit their compositions in order to improve the quality of their final written work. Unfortunately, the conclusion from a great deal of research is that teaching formal, traditional school grammar does not result in improved student writing. Some research and current expert opinion suggest that teachers should teach the conventions of written English functionally, within the context of meaningful reading and writing. This chapter provided some recommendations for teaching grammar and punctuation functionally. Chapter 9 deals specifically with spelling.

REFERENCES

*Recommended for teachers

International Reading Association and National Council of Teachers of English. (1996). *Standards for the English language arts*. Newark, DE and Urbana, IL: Authors.

*Atwell, N. (1987). *In the middle: Writing, reading, and learning with adolescents*. Portsmouth, NH: Heinemann.

Braddock, R., Lloyd-Jones, R., & Schoer, L. (1963). *Research in written composition*. Urbana, IL: National Council of Teachers of English.

*Calkins, L. M. (1994). *The art of teaching writing*. Portsmouth, NH: Heinemann.

*Graves, D. H. (1994). *A fresh look at writing*. Portsmouth, NH: Heinemann.

Hartwell, P. (1994). Grammar, teaching of. In A. C. Purves (Ed.), *Encyclopedia of English studies and language art*, Vol. 1 (pp. 534–541). New York: Scholastic.

Hillocks, G., Jr. (1986). *Research on written composition: New directions for teaching*. Urbana, IL: ERIC and National Council of Teachers of English.

Hillocks, G., Jr., & Smith, M. W. (1991). Grammar and usage. In J. Flood, J. M. Jensen, D. Lapp, & J. R. Squire (Eds.), *Handbook of research on teaching the English language arts* (pp. 591–603). New York: Macmillan.

Noguchi, R. R. (1991). *Grammar and the teaching of writing: Limits and possibilities*. Urbana, IL: National Council of Teachers of English.

Straw, S. B. (1994). Teaching of grammar. In A. C. Purves (Ed.), *Encyclopedia of English studies and language arts* (pp. 534–538). New York: Scholastic.

Taylor, S. J. (1986). Grammar curriculum—back to square one. *English Journal, 75*(1), 94–98.

*Weaver, C. (1996). *Teaching grammar in context*. Portsmouth, NH: Boynton/Cook.

*Weaver, C. (1998). *Teaching grammar in the context of writing*. In C. Weaver (Ed.), *Lessons to share on teaching grammar in context* (pp. 18–38). Portsmouth, NH: Boynton/Cook.

23 Assessment

COMPETENCY 10.1
Develop and conduct assessments that involve multiple indicators of learner progress.

COMPETENCY 10.2
Administer and use information from norm-referenced tests, criterion-referenced tests, formal and informal inventories, constructed-response measures, portfolio-based assessments, student self-evaluations, work/performance samples, observations, anecdotal records, journals, and other indicators of student progress to inform instruction and learning.

Interpretation

These two competencies focus on assessments and tests, both formal and informal. The first, Competency 10.1, encourages teachers to both develop and conduct assessments that will provide them with a variety of information that they can use to evaluate the progress of the students in their classrooms. The second, Competency 10.2, encourages teachers to administer and use information from norm-referenced and criterion-referenced tests and assessments, and reading inventories, as well as from a number of teacher-organized and classroom-specific measures of student achievement. Furthermore, Competency 10.2 recommends that teachers interpret the information derived from these tests and assessments and use it to determine student progress and learning and to plan instruction. Because these two competencies are so closely associated, we will discuss them together.

Related Research

How to measure and evaluate student achievement, both individually and in groups, is a topic of great interest to teachers, parents, administrators, school board members, reading researchers, and members of the public and their elected representatives at the state and national levels of government. But how to use information from tests and assessments to meet the instructional needs of students is of particular interest to teachers, as well as to the developers of instructional programs.

For a chapter on the assessment of students as they are learning to read, one expert developed the following table that defines some of the audiences concerned with reading assessments and the types of questions members of these various audiences are likely to ask.

It is because so many people are concerned about the achievement of students in U.S. schools that testing and assessment play such an important role in U.S. education. Students are tested and assessed in most of the subjects they encounter in school. In this chapter, however, we focus only on tests and assessments that center on reading.

Although the terms *test* and *assessment* are most often used interchangeably, they are sometimes assigned separate meanings. The term *assessment* is perhaps most often associated with the teacher-developed and usually informal measures of student progress that teachers use to evaluate their students, as well as to plan, and when necessary, change reading instruction so that it more precisely addresses the needs of their students.

Audience	Representative Questions Asked by Audience
Legislators	Are schools meeting state goals and standards? Are particular school districts notable for their levels of performance?
State education department	Are new learning-to-read programs working? Which ones?
Taxpayers	Is our money well spent?
Parents	How is my child doing? What can I do to help my child become a better reader?
School administrators	How are the teachers doing? Is building-wide or district-wide initiative working?
Teachers	Is my instructional optimal? Are students' learning goals met? Is my placement of students accurate? What does this student need in terms of remedial or accelerated curriculum?
Students	What's this thing called reading assessment? What kind of reader am I? How did I do on the assignment? How am I doing on the recent task? How is reading assessment helpful to me in my development as a reader? What have I accomplished, and what do I have to do still?

Afflerbach, 1998, p. 250.

The term *test* is often associated with more formal measures of student achievement, such as commercially developed and scored norm-referenced standardized reading tests. Such tests are given once a year in most U.S. schools. Norm-referenced tests provide scores that indicate how one student's performance compares with that of a representative group of students. Test developers achieve these comparisons by referencing the score of a student taking the test to the scores of a group of students in the "norming" sample. The term *standardized* alludes to the consistent manner in which the tests are given, as well as to the comparison of the scores of students taking the test to the other students who took the test.

Criterion-referenced tests are designed to measure student knowledge of specific content, or to determine if they have met specified criteria in a given subject area, sometimes called "benchmarks." Criterion-referenced tests can be based on criteria set by a classroom teacher, a textbook company, a testing company, a school district, or the state. Rather than comparing a student's score to the norming group, as in a norm-referenced test, a criterion-referenced test compares a student's score to an absolute standard. The numbers of items that the student must answer correctly to meet the criterion for passing is determined—depending on the nature of the test—by the teacher, the district, the testing company, or the state. Some commercially developed criterion-referenced tests provide categories for student performance, for example, "below basic," "basic," "proficient," and "exemplary."

Although the goals and reporting mechanisms for norm-referenced and criterion-referenced tests differ, test developers strive to create tests that are reliable and valid. Two questions (and their answers) seem the best way to explain these terms:

1. Does the test measure what it says it measures? If so, we say it is valid or that it has validity.
2. Does the test consistently measure what it says it measures? If so, then it is reliable and we say it has good reliability (Templeton, p. 565).

The developers of commercially prepared standardized and criterion-referenced tests are not the only test makers concerned with the validity and reliability of their tests. Teachers who develop their own classroom assessments are also concerned that the assessments they develop reflect and measure student achievement and that they do so consistently.

Commercially developed tests and assessments, however, differ in a number of ways from teacher-created assessments. Because commercially developed tests are designed to be used in many classrooms, they are not likely to closely reflect the curriculum of any specific classroom. Student scores on these tests are often used to compare the achievement of students in one classroom with the achievement of students in other classrooms, schools, school districts, and states. Scores on these tests are often used by school administrators and policymakers at the local and state levels to make decisions about, for example, the allocation of Title I funding and the need for intervention programs. In recent years, scores on standardized tests have been used by school administrators as a basis for making decisions about student promotions, summer school eligibility, and assigning students to special education programs. State

Departments of Education often use standardized test data to make decisions to intervene in schools in which the scores of most students are below an acceptable level. It is for these reasons that these tests are sometimes labeled as "high-stakes" tests, in that important decisions about individual students and teachers, school curricula, and state funding are made on the basis of student scores on standardized tests.

A number of educators have expressed concerns about the overuse of standardized tests in U.S. schools. For example, one group of researchers describes four negative consequences that can result from an overreliance on norm-referenced, standardized tests: (1) Standardized tests do not reflect a research-based understanding of reading, particularly higher-order thinking skills; (2) some teachers teach to the tests, thus "narrowing " the classroom curriculum and fragmenting teaching and learning; (3) because information about student performance on norm-referenced tests typically appears long after the tests are administered, teachers and students are made to feel like passive recipients of test information, rather than active participants in an ongoing assessment process; (4) dependency on standardized tests causes teachers and policymakers to rely on only one indicator of student achievement rather than on the multiple indicators that can emerge from classroom-based assessments (Valencia, Hiebert, and Afflerbach, 1994, p. 7).

Concern about the perceived misuses of norm-referenced tests in recent years has led to an interest in the development of an array of different types of classroom-based assessments. In particular, the concern is that standardized norm-referenced tests should not be the sole basis for evaluating student progress and making instructional decisions about students and school programs. Consistent with the concerns of many of the critics of standardized testing, Competency 10.1 specifies that teachers develop and conduct "multiple indicators" of learner progress. This competency stresses the importance of classroom teachers incorporating a variety of measures of student progress, measures that will provide them with many ways to evaluate the reading achievement of their students.

The term *authentic assessment* is often used to describe an approach to assessment that not only focuses on multiple indicators of progress, but also on the use of classroom-based information to make instructional decisions. Proponents of authentic assessment have an interest in involving students in gathering information about their progress and using that information to evaluate and plan their learning. Authentic assessment can take many forms and involve a variety of student responses, thus providing teachers (as well as students and their parents) with a wide array of information. Many of the assessments listed in Competency 10.2 are examples of authentic assessments, for example, portfolio-based assessments, student self-evaluations, work/performance samples, observations, anecdotal records, and journals. Other authentic assessments that could be added to this list include reading logs, student writing folders, scheduled interviews, and records based on cooperative group activities.

A characteristic of all authentic assessments in reading and the language arts is that they are intended to reflect the real tasks of reading and writing rather than more abstract test-taking tasks, such as filling in blanks with one or two words and selecting one correct answer from an array of possible answers. Most supporters of authentic assessment urge caution as teachers consider the development and uses of these assessments in their classrooms. One group stresses the importance of teachers having a philosophy or rationale for selecting which assessments to use and when. They also point to the importance of the "authentic" aspects of these forms of assessment: "The term *[authentic assessment]* is especially appropriate to signify assessment activities that represent the community and workplace, and that reflect the actual learning and instructional activities of the classroom and out-of-school worlds" (Valencia, Heibert, & Afflerbach, 1994, p. 11).

Closely associated with the concept of authentic assessment are "performance assessments," in which students, working either individually or in groups, create products or responses to demonstrate what they have learned. Performance assessments come in many forms, such as writing essays, narratives, expository pieces, letters, mathematical computations, oral presentations, conducting an experiment, or working cooperatively in a group (Winograd & Arrington, 1999).

Performance assessment of reading can, for example, involve discussing or writing about the four most important ideas in a chapter students select from a novel they have read, or entering their responses to a series of related books in their reading logs and then making an oral presentation that compares these responses. In social studies, groups of students can use information from their research on the Nile River to create a topographical map of the Nile Valley. They can then write reports and make presentations about what happens to the river and to the land around it at different times of year. Performance assessments can take only a couple of minutes, for example, "Write three different sentences that contain the word, *temporary*," or, in contrast, can involve projects that students work on over a period of several days.

What Does This Mean for You, the Teacher?

Because Competency 10.1 centers on teachers developing and conducting assessments that will provide multiple indicators of student progress, and a good number of the assessments specified in Competency 10.2 are intended to be teacher-developed assessments, this section emphasizes the assessments that you can develop and conduct in your classroom to help you evaluate student progress and plan instruction. This section also discusses the implications for administering and interpreting standardized and criterion-referenced tests. (The topics are presented in the order they are listed in Competency 10.2.)

Norm-Referenced Tests

These are the "high-stakes tests" that are used to compare the performance of your students with that of a representative sample of students. You can help your students prepare for these tests by giving them practice with the types of test questions they will encounter on the test, for example, showing them how to go about evaluating the possible responses to multiple-choice questions and determining the best choices. (See Chapter 20 for additional information on teaching test taking strategies.)

You will learn about the requirements for administering the tests, most often, from the school principal. For the most part, these tests are sent away to the testing company to be machine scored. It is important to learn how to interpret the tests. Grade equivalents and percentiles are the most common ways of reporting norm-referenced scores, although percentiles have more statistical reliability than grade-equivalent scores. Percentile scores will tell you the percentage of students scoring lower than any given student. (For example, 82 percent of the students taking the test score below a student who is at the 82nd percentile.) You should be prepared to discuss student scores with parents. Student scores on these tests, along with information from classroom-based assessments, can provide you and your school with information that can be used to evaluate your program of reading instruction. This will be done most effectively, however, if you work in cooperation with the teachers and administrators of your school.

Criterion-Referenced Tests

These tests compare student performance with established criteria or standards. Many state tests of reading achievement are commercially developed criterion-referenced tests that are based on the particular standards of a given state. These tests are given in classrooms throughout the state. They may be given in every grade, starting for example, in third grade, or they may be given on a two- or three-year schedule. How can you best prepare your students for these tests? Obviously, it is important that you, their teacher, know the criteria that are the basis of the tests and include instruction that will help your students meet these goals. And, as in preparing students to take norm-referenced tests, it is often useful if you help your students learn to respond to the different forms of questions and prompts used in the test. We will point out, however, that the best preparation for any of these tests is a program of good reading instruction and daily opportunities for extended reading and writing in your classroom.

Informal Reading Inventories (or IRIs)

These commercially developed diagnostic assessments are individually administered. You can use IRIs to learn more about the specific reading strengths and weakness of each of your students; more specifically, you are most likely to use these assessments to evaluate students you are concerned about for grade placement to determine if they need extra instruction, or to determine their eligibility for special programs. Most commercially developed IRIs involve students reading graded sets of word lists and passages and then answering comprehension questions about the passages. When giving an inventory, you can evaluate oral reading fluency, gain information about how the student identifies words, and learn about some of the strategies the student uses to read text. Most inventories also help you identify the level of text the student can read independently. Some IRIs are available independently of any reading program, whereas others accompany basal reading programs. Of course, you can develop your own inventory as you become experienced with the progress of the students in your classroom.

Constructed Response Measures

These tests usually involve students reading a passage and then writing a set of short answers in response to a prompt or set of questions about the passage. Constructed-response measures are a common feature of many commercially developed tests. You can help your students learn how to construct responses by giving them practice, beginning with prompts and questions you write about paragraphs on familiar topics. You can then introduce paragraphs that center on less familiar topics and discuss comprehension strategies for understanding the material in preparation for writing responses to prompts and questions.

Portfolios

Portfolios are collections of student work that you and your students use to keep track of and evaluate their learning and progress over time. The portfolios themselves can consist of large file folders, three-ring binders, or boxes. In saying that portfolios should be used to help students express what they are learning and demonstrate what they can do, one reading educator (Templeton, 1995) urges that portfolios contain products that represent students' best work as well as information about the process they use to produce these products. He writes: "The defining essence or nature of the portfolio is self-expression and self-reflection, interpretation, and analysis" (Templeton, 1995, p. 557). You can help your students learn to select pieces of work for their portfolios that reflect their growth as readers and writers. In regularly scheduled conferences during which you go over the portfolios of individual students, you can help each student develop an appreciation for his or her strengths and a sensitivity to weaknesses. And you will learn more about the effectiveness of your classroom instruction and how to modify that instruction to meet the needs of your students.

Student Self-Evaluation

In collecting evidence of their achievements in portfolios, students are encouraged to be reflective about their learning. You can help your students evaluate their learning and their progress in many ways. Some of these are direct, for example, you can provide students with checklists and surveys that focus on self-evaluation. Or you can ask them to write open-ended statements about their perceptions of their progress. Such documents can also serve as a complement to your own assessments of the progress of your students.

Work/Performance Samples

Work/performance samples are most often the products of specific assignments you give to individual students or groups of students. These samples can take many forms, for example, writing projects, drawings or other graphic displays, audiotapes of oral reading, and videotapes of reading discussions. You can urge your students to include some work/performance samples in their portfolios.

Observations and Anecdotal Records

Kid-watching is a term often used to describe the practice of systematically observing students as they are engaged in reading and writing tasks and recording these observations. You may decide to write anecdotal records to describe specific events that individual students or groups of students engage in, or, perhaps, individual students for whom some specific behavioral information is needed for placement in special programs. Of course, you make informal observations about the responses of your students on a daily basis, and make instructional decisions based on these observations. But more deliberate observations and anecdotal records will permit you to reflect on and interpret the progress and problems of your students over time. These records can provide you with some additional information on which to base student grades.

Journals

Journals that students make entries in regularly can be an important means of their learning about the relationships between reading and writing, as well as gaining an appreciation for the importance of their own written expression. When you emphasize journal writing in your classroom, you also emphasize your students' personal involvement in their own learning. Your students can make entries in their journals for many reasons. They can write in response to prompts that you give them; they can write on their own to reflect on what they have been thinking, observing, and reading; they can make lists of things they want to do, books they want to read, and topics they want to learn and write about. They can write out plans for reports they will create. They can write drafts of their own stories and poems.

You will want to go over student journals on a regular basis so that you can become aware of the strengths and weaknesses of their written work. You will find that, by having your students make regular entries in their journals, you will be provided with a basis for evaluating student growth and achievement over time. Additionally, you may choose to do dialogue journals with your students, in which you regularly write personal responses to them. Some teachers and students use the Internet to engage in written dialogues. Some teachers also keep journals in which they record notes about their own teaching, observations about their students, and ideas and plans for improved instruction. (See Chapter 2 for an additional discussion of journals.)

Some Other Indicators of Student Progress to Inform Instruction and Learning

There are many other forms of testing and assessment that are not specifically listed in Competency 10.2. We will mention only three.

Attitude Surveys.   These surveys, often available in methods textbooks or teacher-developed, are given orally or in written form, depending on the age and achievement of the students. Attitude surveys can help you gather information about, for example, your students' knowledge of reading mechanics or their interest and motivation in learning to read.

Placement Tests.   Many commercially developed and organized programs of reading instruction contain placement tests to determine the reading grade level of students. You can follow the directions for giving these tests and use the information from student performance on the tests to place children in a program of instruction. Keep in mind, however, that many students respond to instruction more positively than they respond to a placement test given at the beginning of the school year. Your daily observations of your students' performance are more valid than scores on a placement test. On the other hand, keep good records of the performance of your students on the tests. You may find them helpful when you evaluate their progress during the school year.

Progress or Unit Tests.   These tests are based on the content of basal reading programs and are intended to provide teachers with information about the achievement of the students as they progress through a given basal reading program. In that they assess what students are being taught, they can be considered criterion-referenced tests. If you, or your school, decides to use these tests, you should follow the directions for giving them and use the results to help you make instructional decisions. Some progress tests offer suggestions for extra instruction for students who exhibit problems on the tests. If you keep good records of student achievement on unit tests, you can use them as one of your indicators of learner progress.

Summary

The testing and assessment of what students are learning about reading and writing plays an important role in U.S. education. Most school districts and states require some form of standardized norm-referenced or criterion-referenced testing of students in public schools. In response, perhaps, to an overdependence on data from these "high-stakes" tests, the IRA competencies on assessment stress the importance of teachers being able to develop and conduct assessments that will provide them with multiple indicators of student progress. The term *authentic assessment* is used to describe assessments that directly relate to the kinds of reading and writing activities that occur in classrooms and the real world. The authentic assessment activities described in this chapter are examples of the kinds of classroom assessments that teachers are encouraged to develop and use to evaluate the progress of their students and to make instructional plans and decisions.

REFERENCES

Afflerbach, P. P. (1998). Reading assessment and learning to read. In J. Osborn & F. Lehr (Ed.), *Literacy for all*. New York: Guilford.

Templeton, S. (1995). *Children's literacy: contexts for meaningful learning*. Boston, MA: Houghton Mifflin.

Valencia, S. W., Hiebert, E. F., & Afflerbach, P. P. (Eds.). (1994). *Authentic reading assessment: Practices and possibilities*. Newark, DE: International Reading Association.

Winograd, P., & Arrington, H. J. (1999). Best practices in literacy assessment. In L. B. Gambrell, L. M. Morrow, S. B. Neuman, & M. Pressley (Eds.), *Best practices in literacy instruction*. New York: Guilford.

24 Recommendations

The IRA *Standards* include many reading competencies that are crucial for reading professionals to know and apply. In *Reading Instruction and Assessment: Understanding the IRA Standards*, we have tried to define and elaborate these competencies. Besides explaining the existing IRA *Standards*, however, we developed some recommendations that we think would strengthen the next revision of the IRA *Standards*. In this chapter, we offer three sets of recommendations: (1) make some competencies more specific; (2) subdivide some competencies that are too broad; and (3) add some competencies.

Recommendation 1

Make some competencies more specific. We recognize that the authors of the IRA *Standards* intentionally avoided being too specific in the belief that "Educators at state and local levels should have the right to define curriculum and determine the best instruction for their students" (p. 1). Nonetheless, to be truly helpful to the intended audiences of the IRA *Standards*, we think some *Standards* need to be more specific than they currently are.

Be More Sensitive to Developmental Level

One suggestion for increasing specificity is to have the competencies reflect the fact that the language arts are developmental processes. Part I of the IRA *Standards* begins with "Core beliefs about the knowledge base for teaching and learning that inform the *Standards for Reading Professionals*." One of these core beliefs is: "The language arts are complex behaviors that develop over time; individual learners do not progress at the same rate in the same ways" (p. 1). Yet this belief is not evident in the competencies described in the category of Instruction and Assessment that is the focus of this book.

The current IRA *Standards* identify teachers at three levels: early-childhood (preschool–grade 3); elementary school (grades K–5); and middle and secondary school (grades 6–12). In addition, the *Standards* designate four levels of proficiency associated with each competency: Awareness ("has awareness of the different aspects of literacy development and related teaching procedures"); Basic Understanding ("has knowledge about specific instructional tasks and has fundamental proficiency in the performance of those tasks for the aspect of literacy development"); Comprehensive Understanding ("is able to apply proficiently broad, in-depth knowledge of the different aspects of literacy development in instructional settings"); Not applicable (p. 8). We do not think that these designations are sufficient to capture the complex developmental nature of reading and writing. The grade-level designations are too broad, and the levels of proficiency are too vague and appear to be assigned rather arbitrarily.

In the list of competencies, very little mention is made of developmental levels. Developmental issues are included only in one section, Knowledge and Beliefs About Reading. Here, only two out of thirty competencies acknowledge development: Competency 2.7, "understand emergent literacy and the experiences that support it," and Competency 3.3, "understand that spelling is developmental and is based on students' knowledge of the phonological system and of the letter names, their judgements of phonetic similarities and differences, and their ability to abstract phonetic information from letter names." In the section Instruction and Assessment, no competencies mention development. We suggest that reading professionals must not only "know and believe" that all the language arts are developmental, but must also possess the skill to assess the developmental levels of their students. In addition, they must know how to provide appropriate instruction based on their assessment.

We thought the three competencies related to writing were especially lacking in sensitivity to developmental issues. From the current IRA *Standards*, one might conclude that a "comprehensive understanding" of writing instruction is not required until middle and secondary school. Research, however, has consistently emphasized the relationship of reading and writing and the importance of writing in learning to read. We suggest that reading professionals at all levels, but especially at the early childhood and elementary school levels, need a "comprehensive understanding" of writing. We have more to say on this point in our second major recommendation.

One document that could provide a model for developmentally sensitive competencies for instruction and assessment is "Learning to read and write: Developmentally appropriate practices for young children" (National Association for the Education of Young Children, 1998). This document is a joint position statement of the International Reading Association and the National Association for the Education of Young Children. It was adopted by both of these organizations in May 1998. The position statement includes recommended teaching practices for preschoolers, kindergartners, first, second, and third graders. The recommendations are quite specific. For example, preschool teachers are encouraged to "talk about letters by name and sounds" and "encourage children to experiment with writing," while kindergarten teachers are urged to "help children to segment spoken words into individual sounds and blend the sounds into whole words (for example, by slowly writing a word and saying its sound)." We believe such specific recommendations, which are meant to be "illustrative, not exhaustive" (NYAEC, 1998, p. 46) would be more helpful to reading professionals. Even though developmental level is certainly not synonymous with grade level, we suggest that more specific guidance for reading professionals at different grade levels is more helpful than providing proficiency level designations for broad grade-level categories.

Decide on an Appropriate Level of Detail and Be Consistent across Competencies

A few IRA competencies are quite detailed and specific. For example, in the subcategory of Assessment, Competency 10.2 lists very specific types of assessment that reading professionals should know how to administer and use. In other competencies, however, very little detail is provided; furthermore, in some cases the examples that are provided seem to us be unrepresentative of the competency. An example is Competency 7.1: "Provide direct instruction and model when and how to use multiple comprehension strategies, including retelling." As we discuss in Chapter 11, research has identified a number of comprehension strategies. We believe that the IRA *Standards* should include *all* of the research-validated strategies rather than, for no discernible reason, singling out one strategy.

Another example of inadequate and unrepresentative detail occurs in Competency 5.5: "Provide opportunities for creative and personal responses to literature, including storytelling." We suggest that the recommendations we offer regarding reader response in Chapter 2 reflect a more appropriate level of detail. They include providing various forms of written and oral response, as well as response through the expressive arts.

Recommendation 2

Subdivide some competencies that are too broad. Related to our recommendation that the IRA *Standards* should include an appropriate level of detail is our suggestion that some competencies are too broad and need to be subdivided into more focused competencies. An example is Competency 7.5: "Ensure that students can use various aspects of text to gain comprehension, including conventions of written English, text structure and genres, figurative language, and intertextual links." "Aspects of text" is a very large category. Some examples of "aspects of text" are provided, but even some of these examples, such as "text structure and genres," are quite broad. In Chapter 15, we tried to elaborate on the meaning of text structures and genres, but we did not include some genre-related concepts that many would consider critical to reading, such as "literary concepts" used in discussions of literary response and analysis. These literary concepts include, for example, (1) the analysis of characters, including their traits, motivations, conflicts, points of view, relationships, and changes they undergo; (2) how the author's perspective or point of view affects the text; (3) the analysis of story plot, setting, and problem resolution; (4) the recognition and interpretation of literary devices such as flashback, foreshadowing, and symbolism; (5) the recognition of how style, tone, and mood contribute to the effect of the text; (6) the ways in which irony, tone, mood, the author's style, and the "sound" of language achieve specific rhetorical or aesthetic purposes or both; and (7) the identification of recurring themes across works. We are not suggesting that the IRA *Standards* should include this level of detail. Rather, we are suggesting that "ensuring that students can use various aspects of text," even with a few examples, may be far too broad a competency. We recommend separate competencies for different aspects of text, including literary concepts.

Recommendation 3

Add some competencies. While the IRA *Standards* are fairly comprehensive, we think some important competencies were omitted from the category of Instruction and Assessment. We briefly discuss our recommendations for additional competencies below.

Include Greater Attention to the Other Language Arts

Although titled *Standards for* Reading *Professionals*, another of the core beliefs listed in Part I of the document is: "The language arts—reading, writing, speaking, listening, viewing, and representing visually—are interrelated; they are rarely used in isolation, and they tend to be mutually reinforcing as students learn and use them" (p. 1). Based on our knowledge of the research, we heartily concur with this statement. Although the interrelatedness of the language arts is a core belief of the authors of the IRA *Standards*, it is not strongly reflected in the competencies for Instruction and Assessment. Only one competency specifically mentions the language arts, Competency 5.6: "Promote the integration of language arts in all content areas." The only language art specifically included in Instruction and Assessment besides reading is writing. Only three competencies are listed in the subcategory of writing, and none mentions a relationship to reading.

Because the language arts are interrelated and mutually reinforcing, we believe it may not be appropriate to even attempt to target standards solely for reading. Teachers need to know how to use the fact that the language arts are interrelated and mutually reinforcing to enhance literacy instruction. We recommend that the next version of the IRA *Standards* include greater attention to all the language arts in the category of Instruction and Assessment.

Include More Emphasis on the Importance of Volume of Reading

A particularly compelling research finding is that the volume, or amount, that children read is related to the development of their cognitive abilities. Volume of reading promotes general knowledge, vocabulary growth, and reading comprehension (Cunningham & Stanovich, 1998). According to these authors:

> we should provide all children, regardless of their achievement levels, with as many reading experiences as possible. Indeed, this becomes doubly imperative for precisely those children whose verbal abilities are most in need of bolstering, for it is the very

act of reading that can build those capacities. An encouraging message for teachers of low-achieving students is implicit here. We often despair of changing our students' abilities, but there is at least one partially malleable habit that will itself develop abilities—reading! (pp. 14–15).

This conclusion is emphasized again in the report of the National Reading Panel, which claims that there are hundreds of studies that

> find that the best readers read the most and that poor readers read the least. . . . It appears—from the correlations—that the more you read, the better your vocabulary, your knowledge of the world, your ability to read, and so on (2000, p. 3–21).

We think this statement, supported as it is by considerable research, is an extremely important message to convey to reading professionals, perhaps more important than many of the other IRA competencies. The message about the importance of volume of reading may be implicit in some of the IRA competencies in the subcategory "Creating a Literate Environment," but we believe the importance of promoting volume of reading needs to be much more explicit by including it as a separate competency in the category of Instruction and Assessment.

How to most effectively increase the amount of reading students engage in is not a simple matter. The National Reading Panel points to the lack of evidence of effectiveness of some of the most commonly used classroom procedures for increasing the amount of student reading. These procedures include SSR (Silent Sustained Reading), DEAR (Drop Everything and Read), and Million Minutes. The Panel urges that further studies need to monitor the amount of time students spend reading, and that more careful work needs to be done to determine the factors that contribute to greater reading by some students.

As part of emphasizing both the complexities and the importance of volume of reading, we think the IRA *Standards* should include a recommendation about reading aloud to students. Even before children can read independently, they can accrue the cognitive benefits of reading by being read to. One of the most compelling and oft-cited quotes from *Becoming a Nation of Readers* is "the single most important activity for building the knowledge required for eventual success in reading is reading aloud to children" (Anderson, Hiebert, Scott, & Wilkinson, 1985, p. 23). The value of reading aloud to students does not disappear once they can read independently. For this reason, we recommend that the IRA *Standards* emphasize both reading aloud to students and promoting independent reading in a competency related to the importance of volume of reading.

Include the Topics of Print Awareness, Phonological Awareness, and Fluency

We were surprised to find these three topics absent from the IRA's listing of competencies. In this section, we will briefly discuss each of them and their importance to a program of reading instruction, particularly in the classrooms of kindergarten and first-grade students.

Print Awareness.   Print awareness, which includes knowledge of the alphabet, is an essential component of children's emerging literacy. In fact, children's knowledge of letter names is one of the two best predictors of their success in learning to read. (The other major predictor is phonemic awareness, which we discuss in the next section.)

The topic of print awareness not only encompasses children's knowledge of the alphabet, but also their understandings of the functions and characteristics of the print that they see on signs, labels, lists, and, of course, in books and other print materials. In addition to letter-learning activities, print awareness activities typically help children acquire some essential information about books, that, for example, the title page contains information about the author and illustrator, as well as the title of the book; that the print represents speech; that the lines of print are read from left to right and from top to bottom; that printed words are separated by spaces.

Because of their varying home experiences, students enter school with vastly differing amounts of information about the functions of print and the letters of the alphabet. When they enter kindergarten, some children thoroughly understand the uses of print and the characteristics of books. In addition, they can identify, say, and write all of the letters of the alphabet, both upper and lower case. These children are not candidates for extensive instruction in print awareness. But other, less knowledgeable children, will benefit from activities that develop their print awareness and alphabetic knowledge. In her discussion of young children who have not had many experiences with books and the letters of the alphabet, Adams warns, "For these children, there is not a classroom moment to waste" (1990, p. 48).

Aspects of print awareness have been discussed in the literature of beginning reading instruction for a number of years (for example, Durkin, 1983; Duffy & Roehler, 1986). The authors of *Preventing Reading Difficulties* advise that: "Kindergarten instruction should be designed to provide practice with the sound structures of words, the recognition and production of letters, knowledge about print concepts, and familiarity with the basic purposes and mechanisms of reading and writing" (Snow, Burns, & Griffin, 1998, p. 322).

We suggest that the next version of the IRA *Standards* include print awareness and alphabetic knowledge with its competencies related to beginning reading instruction.

Phonemic Awareness.   Phonemic awareness instruction involves the understanding that, in addition to conveying meaning, spoken words consist of a stream of sounds that can be separated. The separated sounds of words are called *phonemes*. It is important to keep in mind that phonemic awareness is not phonics. Phonics instruction focuses on the *relationships* between sounds and letters. Phonemic awareness instruction focuses on the *sounds* that comprise spoken words, and how to separate, or segment, those sounds. Along with knowledge of the alphabet, understanding that spoken words are sequences of phonemes is one of the most reliable predictors of students' success in learning to read and write in an alphabetic writing system.

The role of phonemic awareness in learning to read has been established over the past two decades in a number of studies (e.g., Adams, 1990; Juel, 1988, 1994; Snow, Burns, & Griffin, 1998; National Reading Panel, 2000). Related to, and preceding phonemic awareness, is what some researchers describe as a set of four phonological understandings: Over time, children become aware (1) that the stream of speech they hear and speak is composed of separate words, (2) that words are composed of syllables, (3) that some words rhyme, and, finally—and this is the realm of phonemic awareness—(4) that words are comprised of phonemes that can be segmented. For example, the beginning, middle, and ending sounds of one-syllable words can be segmented from the whole word, identified, and put back together, or blended, to form the word. Students combine their knowledge of sounds with their knowledge of letters in order to read.

Preventing Reading Difficulties lists a number of phonemic awareness accomplishments for kindergarten students, for example, "uses phonemic awareness and letter knowledge to spell independently" and " demonstrates understanding that spoken words consist of a sequence of phonemes" (Snow, Burns, & Griffin, 1998, p. 80). The report also recommends that first-grade instruction be designed to provide "specific instruction and practice with sound structures that lead to phonemic awareness . . ." (p. 322).

Another group of researchers writes:

> Unfortunately, phonemic awareness does not come naturally. Achieving it demands that a child attend to the form, rather than the meaning, of speech. This is difficult because our natural inclination is to attend to the meaning. Thus even those children who arrive at school with well-developed oral language may not have developed phonemic awareness. Phonemic awareness is not necessary for speaking or for listening, but it is vital to reading (Graves, Juel, Graves, 1998, p. 96).

In pointing out that phonemic awareness does not come naturally, these researchers also point to the difficulty of teaching phonemic awareness and maintain that some children will need a good deal of assistance in gaining this understanding.

Most recently, the National Reading Panel (2000) evaluated the evidence supporting the need for phonemic awareness instruction. In summarizing the evidence that supports the inclusion of phonemic awareness instruction in programs of beginning reading instruction, members of the Panel formulated a set of questions: "Can phonemic awareness be taught? Does phonemic awareness instruction assist children in learning to read? Does phonemic awareness instruction assist children in learning to spell? Are the results ready for implementation in the classroom?" (National Reading Panel 2000, 2-5–2-6). Although the Panel's answer to each of these questions is "Yes," their cautions stipulate that phonemic awareness instruction is "a means rather than an end" (National Reading Panel, 2000, p. 2-6), in that its value is helping students understand and use the alphabetic system to read and write. They further caution that, in emphasizing phonemic awareness, it is important that teachers not overlook the need to teach letters as well (p. 2-33).

We suggest that the next version of the IRA *Standards* include a competency on phonemic awareness among its competencies related to beginning reading instruction.

Fluency. Adams nicely describes the importance of fluent reading: "Perhaps the single most striking characteristic of skillful readers is the speed and effortlessness with which they can breeze through text" (1990, p. 19). She then justifies the importance of this ability: "Only if your ability to recognize and capture the meanings of the words is rapid, effortless, and automatic, will you have available the cognitive energy and resources upon which comprehension depends" (p. 20).

The term *fluency* is often used to describe a student's ability to read accurately, at a reasonable rate, with attention to punctuation, and with good phrasing and expression. The relationship of the fluent reading of the words in a passage to the comprehension of the passage is well established and is based on the fact that human attention is limited. Fluent readers devote little attention to identifying most of the individual words in a passage, and, therefore, can focus most of their attention to the meanings of the sentences and the paragraphs they are reading. On the other hand, poor readers—whose reading can be characterized as slow, halting, and inaccurate— typically must devote a great deal of attention to the identification of many of the words they encounter, and, thus, have only limited attention to devote to the development of comprehension (Adams, 1990; Pikulski, 1988; Stanovich, 1986).

As they acquire and develop reading skill, many first- and second-grade students gain fluency without any special instruction. For some students, however, extra practice that is directed at the development of fluency will contribute to their ability to quickly identify words and better comprehend what they read.

Fluency practice almost always involves the repeated reading of carefully selected passages. Repeated reading can take many forms. It can be as simple as having the students read and reread passages from their daily reading assignment to their teacher, a student partner, a classroom aide, or a classroom volunteer. Other procedures for increasing the amount of fluency practice include "choral reading," "whisper reading," and "echo reading." More elaborate procedures for increasing fluency involve charting changes in the rate and accuracy of student reading. When charted information is kept at regular intervals during the school year, students benefit from looking at this evidence of their gains in reading rate and the accuracy with which they identify words. They can see evidence of their increasing fluency.

Of considerable importance to successful repeated reading practice is the selection of passages for the students to read. Practice passages should be neither too difficult nor too easy. There are three levels of difficulty of student reading materials: (1) independent level—the highest level at which students can read easily and fluently without assistance, with few errors in word recognition, and with good comprehension and recall; (2) instructional level—the highest level at which students can do satisfactory reading provided that they receive preparation and supervision from a teacher, errors in word recognition are not frequent, and comprehension and recall are satisfactory; (3) frustration level—the level at which students' reading skills break down, fluency disappears, errors in word recognition are numerous, comprehension is faulty, recall is sketchy, and signs of emotional tension and discomfort become evident. Obviously, the passages selected for fluency practice should never be at the frustration level, but should alternate between the instructional and independent levels.

The importance of the development of fluency is also acknowledged in the report of the National Reading Panel. In reporting on the importance of teachers supporting fluency development in young readers, the National Reading Panel poses several questions: "Are guided oral reading procedures effective in improving reading fluency and overall reading achievement? Is there evidence that encouraging children to read on their own is effective in increasing reading fluency and overall reading achievement? Can fluency be encouraged through instructional procedures? Is it important to increase fluency? Are these results ready for implementation in the classroom?" (2000, pp. 3-3–3-4). The Panel's answer to each of these questions is "yes," but it cautions teachers to understand that word recognition accuracy is not the point of reading instruction, and that fluency "represents a level of expertise beyond word recognition accuracy, and that reading comprehension may be aided by fluency" (p. 3-3).

Given the importance of fluency and the benefits to many children of repeated reading practice, we recommend that the next version of the IRA *Standards* contain a competency devoted to the development of reading fluency.

Include More Competencies Related to Beginning Writing

The three writing competencies included in Instruction and Assessment concern process writing and writing conventions. We believe, however, that more attention needs to be given to the development of writing because the interrelationship and mutual reinforcement of reading and writing are particularly strong in the early stages of both processes. As discussed in Chapter 9, children acquire knowledge of the alphabet system through writing as well as through reading.

We suggest that the next version of the IRA *Standards* needs to give more attention to beginning writing. As a minimum, we think it is important to recommend that reading professionals: (1) offer children opportunities to explore the relationship between reading and writing; (2) provide children with regular opportunities to express themselves in writing without undue emphasis on correct spelling and handwriting; and (3) help children understand that writing has a real purpose (NYAEC, 1998).

A Final Note

Developing standards for any discipline is a difficult task. It is especially difficult in the field of reading, where controversy is the norm: Researchers and practitioners often have different interpretations of research findings and hold competing beliefs about reading instruction. We therefore commend and thank the Professional Standards and Ethics Committee of the International Reading Association for their diligence and perseverance in developing *Standards for Reading Professionals, Revised*, a document that identifies many important competencies for reading professionals.

Standards are never "done," however. The development of standards is a process of continuous refinement. Standards are added, deleted, or modified as new research becomes available, as new theories offer different lenses for interpretation, and as classrooms, students, and teachers change. We hope our interpretation of the current IRA *Standards* related to Instruction and Assessment has contributed to readers' understanding of the competencies. We also hope that our recommendations will be taken into consideration for the next revision of the IRA *Standards for Reading Professionals*.

REFERENCES

Adams, M. J. (1990). *Beginning to read: thinking and learning about print—a summary*. University of Illinois at Urbana-Champaign: Center for the Study of Reading.

Anderson, R. C., Hiebert, E. H., Scott, J. A., & Wilkinson, I. A. G. (1985). *Becoming a nation of readers: The report of the Commission on Reading*. University of Illinois at Urbana-Champaign: Center for the Study of Reading.

Cunningham, A. E., & Stanovich, K. E. (1998). What reading does for the mind. *American Educator, 22*(1&2), 8–15.

Duffy, G. G., & Roehler, L. J. (1986). *Improving classroom reading instruction*. New York: Random House.

Durkin, D. (1983) *Teaching them to read*. Boston, MA: Allyn & Bacon.

Graves, M. F., Juel, C., & Graves, B. G. (1998). *Teaching reading in the 21st century*. Boston, MA: Allyn & Bacon.

Juel, C. (1994). *Learning to read and write in one elementary school*. New York: Springer Verlag.

Juel, C. (1998). Learning to read and write: A lognitudinal study of fifty-four children from first through fourth grade. *Journal of Educational Psychology, 80*, 437–447.

National Association for the Education of Young Children. (1998). Learning to read and write: Developmentally appropriate practices for young children. *Young Children, 53*(4), 30–46.

National Reading Panel. (2000). *Teaching children to read: An evidence-based assessment of the scientific research literature on reading and its implications for reading instruction*. Washington, DC: National Institute of Child Health and Human Development.

Pikulski, J. J. (1988). Questions and answers. *The Reading Teacher, 42*(2), 159.

Stanovich, K. E. (1986). Matthew effects in reading: Some consequences of individual differences in the acquisition of literacy. *Reading Research Quarterly, 21*(4), 360–407.

Snow, C. E., Burns, M. S., & Griffin, P. (Eds.). (1998). *Preventing reading difficulties in young children*. Washington, DC: National Academy Press.

INDEX